LETTERS

Library and Archives Canada Cataloguing in Publication

Beorse, Bryn, 1896-1980
    Letters : Shamcher Beorse and Carol Sill, 1974-1977 / selected and edited by Carol Sill.

ISBN 978-0-9781705-5-4

    1. Beorse, Bryn, 1896-1980--Correspondence. 2. Sill, Carol--Correspondence. 3. Mystics--United States--Correspondence. 4. Sufis--United States--Correspondence. 5. Sufis--Canada-- Correspondence. 6. Sufism. 7. Spiritual life--Sufism. 8. Teacher-student relationships--Religious aspects--Sufism. I. Sill, Carol II. Title. III. Title: Shamcher Beorse and Carol Sill, 1974-1977.

BP189.6.B46 2011   297.4'4   C2011-907251-3

Cover design: Diane Feught

© copyright Carol Sill, 2011
Alpha Glyph Publications, Ltd., Vancouver BC
Printed and bound in the United States

http://letters.shamcher.com

LETTERS

SHAMCHER BEORSE AND CAROL SILL
1974-1977

A SUFI CORRESPONDENCE
Selected and Edited by Carol Sill

Toward the One,

The Perfection of Love, Harmony and Beauty,

The Only Being,

united with all the illuminated souls

who form the embodiment of the Master:

The Spirit of Guidance.

INTRODUCTION

Much of Sufi teaching is deeply and universally based in a particular beautiful relationship between teacher and pupil. For the pupil, the presence of a friend or teacher catalyzes an experience which is at the heart of the Sufi path, the awakening of the sleeping soul to realization. These letters form an intimate document of one such relationship.

Murshid Shamcher Beorse was just a name on a list when I began corresponding with him in 1974. I was immediately thrown into the mystical realms through our contact. He was insistent that he was not or never would be a "teacher", very non-hierachial in approach. I exploded in his presence: the journey had begun! As this happened mainly through the mail and in the air, it is all documented here – in real time. Soon I was swept into the world of the Sufis, meeting interesting people who were developed in extraordinary ways, all the while coming closer to understanding my self.

These letters speak of the extraordinary love between Sufis – that love of God through one another. I trust that you can understand their mysticism – the winding paths of love, the realm of exquisite sentiment pushed past all limits. Rather than letting love narrow the universe to the points of two individuals, two individuals expand through love. Shamcher taught me to grow love wider than all creation, and to feed all in fierce expansive compassionate understanding.

Conventional understanding can only help to a certain point, so I encourage you to simply leap in and read this book as it was written – not as a book but as a correspondence of the soul. There I was - a beginner on the spiritual path. Fly along as Shamcher guides me through the winding routes of Love's progress, growth and development.

Sharing these letters is both intensely personal and immensely impersonal. On the surface, they seem to chronicle a common enough love-story but they actually reveal an extraordinary tale: the seed of humanity's development is hidden here. As the tree is contained in the seed, so the full flower of this understanding and its fruit are contained in these letters. The seeds are advice intended for my particular personality. For those who can see behind the personal individual advice, this is a universal story, another revelation of the unfolding of the soul to begin life's work.

We corresponded weekly, sometimes daily, through years until Shamcher's passing in 1980. Naturally, I kept and treasured all his letters to me, but what I didn't know was that he kept all mine to him, and copies of

1

every letter he sent out.

At one point in this correspondence relationship he mailed all my letters back to me, with copies of his own, asking me to put them into a book. I was overwhelmed, but as I put them together, the form of his teaching, my growth, our relationship and the universal love of the Sufis took shape before my eyes.

To my knowledge there are few contemporary western Sufi epistolary books available, what I believe is called "malfuziat" in the east – the letters of a Murshid to a Mureed.

This book is part of Shamcher's legacy. He knew it at the time he told me to publish these letters. It exists not so much as my own story but more as a way of contact with him. His approach may be more relevant now than ever.

What is in this approach? Freedom of the soul and the immense power of love to transform all walks of life from highest to lowest. Not a monastic path, but right down in the dirty worlds of economics and energy, of politics and education. Every morning, early, before the busy world began its movements, he sat in meditation, turning the spheres from nothing to a tiny sound to the vastness of the multiplicity we call the universe, and beyond. With simplicity he understood and resonated the new physics, the scientific approach, integrating the stuff of the Western mind with the ancient teachings of yoga and Sufism.

I came to him open, and broken, transformed and still in shock from the sudden death of my 7 year old son, knowing that if I didn't find a teacher and a path to truth that I would go mad. He guided me with love and subtle communications across the deepest darkest waters of fear and death's misunderstood meanings. He was a lens that reflected the Self to me so I could learn to save my own life.

It has taken me so long to publish this book, as he had wished, because it took me decades to understand that this book is a means for Shamcher's approach to be seen and felt. Shamcher's views were unique, idiosyncratic and solely his own. He encouraged the same independent thought in his few pupils, who now are part of various Sufi organizations and no-organizations. For me, knowing him was the relationship of a lifetime, the ultimate teacher-pupil bond played out at first in the most beautiful correspondence. I hope that my profound and transformative experience in meeting him can be a door or gateway for you to sense or glimpse the presence of that universal guiding lifeflow that Shamcher was engaged with almost all the time. In him it revealed itself through economics, energy and his scientific engineering efforts.

He was as close to each person who came to him as they would permit. Uncensored. Not so much physically, but in a way he called "infeeling". Some found this shocking, unwanted. Both men and women often cried when they met with him. He joked, "I must have been terribly disappointing to them, they burst into tears." He knew this force was in play, whatever name we gave it, and his joy was in that fierce love that awakens humanity, and perhaps could protect the human experiment from self-destruction.

Shamcher's active correspondence was the edge of his influential life. With many in all fields his letters ranged from spiritual intimacy to urging broad global reform. Many others were also close to Shamcher as I was, and their stories, too, are deep and remarkable. He wanted us all to apply our abilities in loving awakened awareness to all aspects of life and work. With that, he thought, there might just be hope for survival.

I tried many times to prepare the book when he was alive, but it was far too personal at that time. After he passed away in 1980, compelled to do something with it, I circulated a limited number of spiral-bound copies. Some people cried when they read them, and said they felt his presence as if the letters had been written directly to them.

In the context of the times of these letters, the psychedelic era had closed, and personal growth, self-awareness and consciousness were highly valued. A time of teachers and gurus, "Be Here Now," Tibetan Buddhism, teachings of Indian yoga: the milieu was hot with intense fervor of seeking. And there was no shortage of gurus, teachers and facilitators to open the awareness of the seekers, most often for a fee. Young people who had passed through the psychedelic portals were looking for stable and lasting higher states of consciousness not dependent on drugs. In stepped the gurus and traditions from the ages.

The Sufism of Inayat Khan had begun to flourish in the West at the beginning of the 20th century, entering at a time of interest in theosophy, eastern mysteries and occult fascinations. Many of Inayat Khan's pupils, first interested in such alternate philosophies, found their home in his "Sufi Message". It is a pure teaching, and was preserved and embodied not simply in his books, esoteric papers and practices, but through his many students and initiates, like Paul Reps, Samuel Lewis and Shamcher Beorse in the US, along with many others in Europe and world-wide, and of course through his sons, Vilayat and Hidayat. In organizations like the Sufi Movement (his original organization) and the Sufi Order (established by Vilayat) the teachings were preserved and given out to new seekers. Many other new groups were also formed over time, with various aspects emphasized or as an answer to a particular need of the day.

To some, these Sufis may seem an odd little fringe association. This work has been decried as a group of "non-Moslem pseudo-Sufis" by orthodox Islamic Sufi groups, no doubt because the Sufi Message of Inayat Khan includes all religions, and is not limited by any creed, any person, any organization. You see, the organization is merely a cover over the enormous love and beauty that these inner teachings offer.

When I first corresponded with Shamcher, I knew he was involved in this lineage, but I had no idea that he had been a pupil of Inayat Khan, whose "Orange Volumes" I had read with such dedicated fascination. He only revealed this to me when we met in person.

In his influence, for 20 years after meeting Shamcher I was very active in establishing and supporting Sufi groups and activities in Canada, creating a space for those with similar interest to come together.

The most vital work, however, happened one to one, not in any group, no matter how devoted or dedicated its members might be. The main living transmission occurs here, rooted in this profoundly personal-universal experience.

A personal "teacher" may not be necessary in these times or in this world. The information is all available, including instructions in even the most esoteric and heretofore secret practices of the inner schools of all traditions. Yet there is an awakening of the heart that is a most beautiful confirmation that occurs between an elder on the path and a new seeker.

Shamcher guided me through his heart and concentration. With his impression reflected in my heart, I functioned beyond my previous limited self. How wonderful, then, to discover that he also was being guided through the impression in his heart. And so forth through this tradition that permits the aspirant to follow and eventually access this full heart-stream right at its source.

This is a tradition of complete and total freedom, once the spark is conveyed. Some shoot out into their lives and professions, into their art or life destiny, others maintain the inner school for new seekers – making a place

4

that retains the deep vibrations of the sacred realms.

Many people who knew Shamcher, even only meeting him once, had this experience of awakening. They tell of how their lives were changed forever due to that contact. More significant than any formal event, the true initiation is an intermolecular quantum event occurring between two beings, happening beyond time and understanding.

All else is a development after the fact, all practices and advice are ways to maintain or engage in the new way of life, to learn to function in this new greater being. It all starts here in the direct contact heart to heart.

Shamcher's influence profoundly impacted every aspect of my life, yet who was he, really? He was a man who had truly lived – travelling far from his native Norway to establish companies and create enterprises in distant lands as far as Borneo (then Dayak-land.) His exploits included working as a jackaroo in Australia, living as a beach bum and journalist in Oceana near Big Sur, writing novels, attending the Khumba Mela, acting as an agent for MI-5, working for the Norwegian underground - ski-guiding escapees from Nazi-occupied Norway to Sweden, participating in a plot to kidnap Hitler, helping restore the Norwegian economy after WWII, seeking buried Nazi gold in China, going on an economic mission to Tunisia for the UN, championing a plan for full employment in the US, and pioneering Ocean Thermal Energy Conversion (OTEC) – benign solar power from the sea which he advocated until the end of his life.

As a pupil of the great mystic Inayat Khan, Shamcher not only travelled widely in his chosen fields of energy and economics, but also in the vast spiritual realms which opened their treasure-houses to him. Having sought a teacher and enlightenment in India, he had returned to Norway disappointed, only to find the great mystic Inayat Khan at his doorstep, so to speak. Asked to translate for him, Shamcher met Inayat at a hotel in Christiania (now Oslo.) This destined contact was the beginning of Shamcher's lifelong engagement with the Sufi effort. Combined with his mystical initiation, his world travels through more than 61 countries became more significant vibrationally, spreading the seeds of the Sufi thought and attitude wherever he travelled.

Shamcher lived intuitively, remaining mostly in the US after WWII. He married his wife Evelyn when he was at the age of 54, and they had two children, Bryn Jr. and Daphne, both of whom live in the Pacific Northwest.

He supported all Sufi efforts, including those of Pir Vilayat in organizing the Sufi Order. Later Shamcher was instrumental in bringing together this organization and the group founded by his friend and fellow pupil of Inayat Khan, Samuel Lewis. This union caused a great flourishing of the Sufi effort in North America through much of the '70s. Described by Pir Vilayat as "the esoteric head of the Sufi Order," Shamcher was still adamant that hierarchies and formal initiations were no longer necessary, and he worked tirelessly to spread these ideas with his friends and pupils, as these letters reveal. He was very supportive of the work of Hidayat Inayat Khan also, as well as other Sufis and great souls who were not affiliated with any particular organization.

His impact as a contemporary Western mystic has remained mostly unknown to the world. He often pointed out that he didn't exist. Shamcher's inner drive that humanity must survive was always uppermost in his life's mission. In his later years he dedicated himself entirely to promoting awareness of the OTEC solar power system, working as emeritus from his office at the University of California Richmond Field Station. This was the man I found myself corresponding with, whose letters were so catalyzing.

Because a great deal of our communication happened without the senses that we normally use to experience life, there is a metaphysical experience to which this book always refers. I still marvel at how Shamcher did this - how did the being of this man reach a stage of evolution that enabled him to communicate fully and completely across distance, across time, and without any physical communication whatsoever? I've come to believe that Shamcher's contact with me was similar to the communication of the loving yogis of the Himalayas who have been in meditation continually throughout the eons of time.

When we set out, I was very young, only 26, and was just beginning my 30s when he passed away six years later. For decades I have been unravelling the secrets that he first awakened in me. His presence gave me strength of purpose and understanding that allowed me to go forward in my spiritual life and also in my daily life to grow and overcome the grief of the loss of our son.

With Shamcher at my side I opened to a world that had been previously closed to me. In this world I was a neophyte, dazzled and astonished as I was learning how to live without my body, and to proceed without my eyes, my ears, and even without my mind.

In this new world all knowledge became intuitively available.

6

Sharing with Shamcher this awareness of eternal life was the experience that we called love. On earth this word has many meanings. In the Sufi tradition, love has always been the word used to describe the impulse that is the creative force of God, Ishq. The limitation of our senses (and of our identification with our senses) keeps us separated from this marvelous world which is our birthright.

Through Shamcher's skilled teaching, I learned to live outside these limitations imposed upon us in life on earth. His presence and help infused and surrounded me in my every action and gesture, and in my communication with every person.

It was truly wonderful to connect with Shamcher and his incredible inheritance from the yogis of the Himalayas, along with all the wise beings who have contributed down through the ages to the exquisite path that is the Sufi caravan.

Publishing these letters 40 years later brings me back to that tremendous gift of truth. I see again the beauty and supreme ecstasy of life lived within the powerful and extraordinary world where the senses do not control all perceptions. My hopes, dreams, and way of life were all formed in those years when he and I were in our deepest contact. I understood that following the path of my soul's inner reality would lead to my true destination in the purpose of my life. I don't regret that I didn't directly fulfill the promise which Shamcher had so clearly seen and which he had with all his heart and being wished for me: for in the end, I made my own path. This had also been his wish.

After meeting Shamcher, I was involved for many years in activities of Sufi traditions and orders, where I met extraordinary, dazzling, beautiful souls living lives that were open and true, following the will of the divine. I love the Sufis and the exquisite teachings of Hazrat Inayat Khan and am so grateful to this beautiful culture of Love, Harmony and Beauty.

Outside the Sufis, I also saw remarkable individuals who had achieved great abilities and intuitive awareness. They hadn't participated at all in any Sufi tradition, yet were freely engaged in the quest. I became more aware that outside formal organizations are many exquisite souls yearning for truth, spontaneously discovering pathways to realization within themselves.

Wasn't this predicted in the *Diamond Sutra*, that souls in the last 500 year period would spontaneously awaken to their own Buddha nature? The further I stepped into the world, the more I realized that every human being is part of this remarkable natural symphony. There are so many people who follow the inner spirit of guidance and help humanity to survive, awaken, and evolve.

Still, as I prepared these letters for publication I wrestled with the paradox of who I was at the time of writing: a young woman in her late 20's, compared with who I am today: a grandmother in her 60's. Then something Shamcher once wrote to me popped into my mind. He said, "The man who first met you at the ferry is now gone," meaning that he had totally changed. And, he implied, it was not only him, I had changed, too. So, the "people" who had met each other that fall of 1974 are both gone, and have already been absorbed into the whole universe; we don't exist.

These letters are not the story of a teacher and his pupil, nor are they a love story; they are simply an artifact - a ticket. A ticket for the train to a destination we are all going to. If you can find even one sentence that can open a new way of seeing or feeling, or can reinforce something that you have experienced in your own life, or perhaps can give you joy, then know that the unseen realm in which Shamcher and I were communicating has a place within your being also.

My letters to him are simply gateways into his being; his letters show how you can sense some of the ways to live both here and there at the same time. Time and space have no meaning here. Death has no dominion here. This place is all there is. Come join us in the play. We are always dancing. At the fireman's ball when I very first met Shamcher I asked him, "Are we creating this or are we perceiving it?" He looked me in the eyes as we danced and said, "Both."

This entire book is a reply to my simple query:

Dear Murshid Shamcher Beorse,
I was given your address by the Sufi Order as I am interested in finding out more about Sufi activities. Will Pir Vilayat be giving any seminars near Seattle? Are there any Sufis in Canada?
I hope to hear from you soon.
Yours truly,
Carol Sill

1974
INITIATION

Sufis are seekers after truth, whether they call themselves Sufis or not. A Sufi is accepted as such as soon as he wants to call himself so, or even if he won't. To me, everyone in the whole wide world may be called a sufi, or, if not, then I may not be one either.

Shamcher

October 18, 1974

Dear Carol Sill,

Thank you for your good letter. Mrs. Charlotte Brautlacht, Atiya her Sufi name, at ...Bothell Washington, telephone ... has the only organized Sufi center at her beautiful home, which you may find by telephoning her so she can give directions. Through my humble assistance she was established here five years ago, initiated by Pir-Vilayat. There is or was another center run by Merlin, who now, however is moving to a Sufi commune in North Carolina.

Atiya's center has regular classes Friday and Tuesday evenings and mostly Universal Worship on Sunday. Guests can sleep in a greyhound-size bus parked on her property and fitted for sleeping quarters. Pir Vilayat has often held seminars in this area. None is planned for the present. His address is .... He is travelling frequently so reply may come late, but if you were planning for him to give a seminar in Alberta, I am sure your letter would be forwarded to wherever he may be.

You are, of course, always welcome to Seattle and will be afforded any amount of time you would require to be fully informed of whatever you have in mind.

Alberta has been on my mind for a good many years, since your first Social Credit Government was installed. I don't know as much as I ought to know about the achievements of this government, I only was familiar with the principle.

I wonder if Edmonton is closer to Cleveland. Cleveland has the most vital Sufi activity, the most loving Sufis. The Cleveland people are very close to and fond of Pir Vilayat, as I am. Atiya in Seattle also was, at first, when I introduced them. At present Atiya, though still a good friend of Pir Vilayat, cannot go along with his policies and is operating on her own. To this she has a perfect right, and I am still her good and close friend, but I wanted to tell you in advance, not knowing how you would react to that.

A Sufi, as you know, is a seeker after truth, and wherever your seeking brings you, that is where you have to go. No one among Sufis is bound to any man, any rule, any organization.

You are most welcome to visit me in our most humble home. Unfortunately we do not have room for any overnight guest. I am working for the navy establishment here and had to take whatever quarters were available. Here is a precious garden but rather a stable for a house.

There are two Sufis located in or near Vancouver, B.C.: Paul Reps, a disciple of Inayat Khan, now mainly teaching Zen, and Reshad Feild, disciple of a Turkish Sufi Boulen, for some months cooperating with Pir-Vilayat, though not now. I don't know their addresses, but if you are interested I shall try my best to find out.

Love,

Shamcher

(I prefer to be addressed just Shamcher, not Murshid Shamcher, or Bryn. The latter on envelopes.)

November 2, 1974

Dear Carol Sill,

You are right, oodles of things came along in addition to and beyond the words in your letter. It caused me at one time to think: Where is Edmonton? Car or air or rail: But then I found I couldn't go, not now at any rate, and besides, would I be able to bring what you wanted?

So to save time and travel expenses for either or both of us, maybe we can first write a little more, and send along lots of thoughts in addition to - and beyond. If you care to, that is. For the two gentlemen in respectively Victoria and Vancouver, B.C. have moved I have been told. One was a Britisher, who started a lecture at the University of Washington by solemnly declaring: "Twelve men rule the world." If there is one thing we don't need at this time it is such dream-world blasts. He is the disciple of a Turkish Sufi teacher and I hope to meet that teacher some time to gauge his mind - and heart. In other words: Not any one claiming to be a teacher, even a Sufi teacher, is a reliable guide or even acceptable as a human being, however certain he may be of his ideas. The other one, who lived in Victoria, was a pupil of Inayat Khan (Pir Vilayat's father) and I am fond of him in a way. After years of ZEN study he became an opponent of Inayat's practices and prayers saying that anything directly taken over from somebody else was no good. This is true for some people but not for all and particularly it is not the teachings or views of Inayat Khan. The Sufis in San Francisco became so angry with him, he called on me to defend him, which of course I did, saying he was perfectly right as far as he himself was concerned and any one feeling the same way. But if he damned all who prayed as they had been taught, his words and acts would gradually lose power.

If you ever go to San Anselmo to see Pir Vilayat there are so many Sufis around you will not run the risk of one-sided and peculiar teachings.

Meanwhile, if you wish to exchange words by mail with one who knows - well, not all, but many, in many countries, and who has a few idiosyncrasies of his own (I have little respect for hierarchies, for example, those represented on earth, worldly or clerical) then come along.

1 love you already, for the warm, large, compassionate thoughts oozing out of your words or sneaking in in spite of them. Tell me about the small things, all you want, what you had for dinner last night, with whom, that ache in your mind and in your neck, your doings during the day, during the evening, the night, the morning, how you sit or stand or lie when you think or even meditate, what thoughts come in, how you get rid of them, how you earn your money or how you get by without.

Love,

Shamcher

P.S. You understand, when I call my thought on hierarchies "idiosyncrasies" that is a play on words. I believe I am more than right. I may not know the exact degree to which this should be reduced or revised, but an awful lot has to be done. In heaven there may be a sort of hierarchy but this is never expressed on earth, not even in the most holy "orders". You find a ditch-digger half hidden in his ditch, I see his heart miles above the bishops and yogacharies.

November 7, 1974

Dear Shamcher,

When I received your letter today, I was filled with such feelings that I can't express it at all on paper. So let me say I was most pleased and would very much like to keep on corresponding with you. Where to begin and what to write?

Please tell me about yourself, more thoughts and feelings, what do you do? Anything...

Sometime, I am sure we will meet person to person, but at this time I feel close to you as if we have been very old friends - only different from that too.

Right now I am renting this typewriter, and do most of my writing on it (but not the poems,) the reason for its rental is part of my work. At this time I am working for the National Film Board putting together a newsprint directory of citizens' groups, and this typewriter was chosen because it spaces letters like typesetting - one less expense. This is only a part time job which

I can do at home - leaving my time my own (to a certain extent) and it's less confusing for me to work from here rather than out in some office. Since I am telling you about my work, please understand that although it is sometimes very satisfying, I can never consider it to be my real life. (The confusion mentioned above is just that - the mixing up of what's real.) Also I am putting together a slide-sound presentation and planning a conference on media and social change. I'm interested in the capabilities of visual media as a means of getting through - but I won't go into that any further here, another letter, if you're interested in my translations of community media theory. (I've never been trained in this, it has just sort of grown and developed as I've been following needs and interests, so in many ways I am naive.)

On the outside, then, that is what I do. On the inside - how can I say - in one day so much can occur, just so much change, it's impossible to write that. With some regularity, I begin each day with a meditation. Often I write, getting through the feelings to some sort of closure, following the closure to new discoveries - then often when all that prose and the clogs in the mind are opened, there will be a poem - I will enclose one for you.

What I find wonderful is: the beginning is always somewhat tentative, I express fears, etc. However it soon just soars of its own accord. I don't often fashion the thoughts afterwards, rewrite or adjust wording. By the time it's through there is another place for my attention to be.

An important part of the story of me has to do with my family. Four months ago our son was drowned. He was seven. It's impossible to tell you this experience in words - but it was painfully the most joyful event, the most deeply meaningful experience - in that wondrous time, we bathed in love; the acceptance, the caring, the true sharing of mind, all barriers between people gone. All that existed was love, caring and sharing. Nothing else was real, only the love. How could I regret such a marvelous gift?

The real work came after the grieving: the work of reconciling everyday life, of living in the new knowledge and working through the post-partum waves of feeling. (So much like a birth. Only three months before I had helped a friend deliver her baby and the feeling was exactly the same between all of us who shared that time - such a crash course in actual existence, the birth and the death, the joy and the pain. And both birth and death hold both at the same time - I wish I could overlap the words, all four into one!)

Cory died in June, and the summer brought "reality" back like a

13

closing iris - the peephole became smaller and I became more easily confused. When I first moved here to Edmonton with my husband, I felt like a new slip, cut off from the old plant, beginning again. I am still going through it, learning a step at a time, learning as I step.

Today it is rainy outside. I will walk to the mailbox in the fur coat my mother gave me - it is old and very warm. This weather is unseasonal, usually at this time there is snow.

There isn't much to tell you, but I want to emphasize the deep FEELING that came through me at the time of reading your letter - I could only call it love for you which seemed to extend very far; so I thank you for that, and hope that you can receive the same from me. Please write back when you have the time. I confess I tend to hold myself back, staying within the confines of "a letter."

I'm thinking of you.

Love,
Carol

November 12, 1974

Dear Carol,

First, that envelope! Of that most dramatic earth event where glaciers swab and grind and reshape rock, like the stream of life grinds and shapes and mollifies my heart - and yours. For our hearts are one now, intertwined, and for the first time in a hundred years, tears come to my eyes; manly tears of joy whenever you sail into my life - by letter or by thought and emotions.

That poem, vibrating, rocking me along, singing me high, tearing me to bits.

What do I do? Almost everything. Some day I may come down from Mount Olympus where you lifted me, and tell. One little thing I have been doing is writing things. One novel about the undergound in Europe (particularly Norway) in World War II was written before many other published books but never came out, because first a British publisher, Ingraham, who loved it and would publish - died. Then Ilsa Lahn, story person in a Hollywood agency wanted it for a movie - then the movies changed their policy. And just now a small NY publisher wrote enthused they wanted it. Then they told me they needed $500 as a contribution to printing. Usually any such contribution is the death knell. Reviewers sniff it out and don't review. But $500 was so modest I acepted, signed contract. Now they bawl me out for "thinking printing can be

14

done for $500." The mother publisher wants $2100, the son $1200. It is not the money so much as the fact they bawl me out for signing the contract *they* proposed. So they said, "OK go and see if you can find a printer who'll do it for that price." So Mothers Print shop in North Carolina quoted: $120 for retyping script for camera printing, $230 for printing 300 copies (213 pages typed on my typewriter, double spaced) and 130 for binding of 300 copies. Altogether 470 - but suddenly Mother's print shop gets a new manager and he quotes: 1300.

And now you write me a letter in exactly the kind of type required for camera printing. So you may know all about these things and have information for me. Do you? I can easily wait with this book. But if somebody wants to offer me a bid for soup to nuts, cost of all until bound books are in hand, I would be much interested. And if you don't want to be bothered with this at all, I love you just as much, just the same, for I cannot help feeling your tremendous pulsating heart rolling in on the mighty air streams from Edmonton, lovely incomparable Carol ....
Shamcher

I loved all you described about the mandala, the symbolic art work, and above all your unusually intuitive following your own precious child into that other world and rejoicing with him... that other world that so many here in this world are afraid of in their strange ignorance.

Undated

Lots of thoughts of Shamcher, all the time, whenever I am not totally occupied with what I am doing - there they are, thoughts of him, of flying to see him, of when I can do it. Though it seems wild and scary to just go hundreds of miles to see someone whom I've never met and in a way don't know at all (for I know nothing about him except that I love him) I know that barring some change in the progression of our relationship, I'll soon be going to visit him.

Already through his letters he has taught me a lot about myself and where I am right now. I don't know what to expect from this, but I do know that something big is going on. My capacity for loving people has increased. Something in me has let go. I know it's not from him, but through him from God. My only doubt is: how much of this am I making up? Are the feelings just my expectation of how it should be, being played out inside me, and I take it to be real? And the answer comes that I must wait and trust whatever experiences come, and follow them step by step.

The only way to discover what is going on is to jump into it and live it. As Gary says: this is the only adventure we've got, this life we live right now. So when I get a letter I trust implicitly and experience honestly all the feelings and changes. It is only afterwards, in the thinking, that 1 feel doubtful.

Last week was spent almost entirely in feelings, very little outside contact with the world. This week will be different, for there is a backlog of work needing to be done; so I must spend less time mooning around, I feel the pressure of work and so know that the way to eliminate it is to do it all and get through it. But truly all I want to do is sit around here thinking of Shamcher. That, I think, is a danger. I really don't want this to become all built up in my head into some idea that it's actually not. All I can say is that there seems to be a friend, a strong relationship begun with someone who can help me to know myself better.

What I want now is to get through this major wall - the wall of thinking - Lately there have been many understandings coming through to me - in words and in images; but I'm always right here. I want to get out of it, I want to dissolve. Whatever the understanding is, it's just an understanding - I'm roving and can't seem to keep this thought clear and the mind wanders to other things, to Shamcher, to whether I should send this to him, whether I should keep the expression of this feeling of cutoffness for the next letter to him - so I know I want to send these feelings to him, I never knew it was this strong!!

SO HELLO DEAR SHAMCHER

This inner writing has turned into a letter to you. As you see from this wild writing, this is all I can do. What do you suppose is happening to me? Is such an experience as this possible through the mail? (But I know that it's not just in the letters.) I feel somewhat foolish sending you reams and reams of paper full of reams of mind wandering but at this point it's all I can do.

Tell me, how do you pronounce your name? How old are you? What is your work? How do you feel in this relationship? Am I learning from you or are you learning from me or is this just us loving each other? It seems as if I've just opened up and opened up and opened up to you.

16

> *I turn to your light*
> *Like a sensitive anemone*
> *As I open*
> *The flowering continues endlessly!*

The feeling which I was attempting to describe in the journal, which was interrupted by the knowing that I must send my entire self to you (what is going on, I ask, over and over again) was this feeling: in every understanding, I am always around, being the understander. There is a separation because I can intellectually understand some very marvelous concepts of the working of the universe, but there I always am, writing it down or thinking it. But one of the understandings is that soon this won't be the case - that me as understander has to go.

Certainly in this relationship we have (or at least from here, I have, - oh, why don't I trust that you respond to me as I do to you? If you didn't, I couldn't be having these feelings.) As I began to tell you before I was darkly interrupted: in this relationship, I am only acting and being. The last thing I can do is understand it.

Where do I go from here? I need to see you - how is this possible? Politeness makes me think that I can't force myself on you, just arrive and phone and expect you to look after me, but I will need you to help me find out where to go. Can you find me a free or inexpensive place to stay? I could leave my work for three days or so and if it's at all possible for us to visit together, please let me know.

I'm overwhelmed at the processes, at this fast change and this writing amazes me - every sentence is a surprise! So the last week in November or the first week in December, these are the times I could come. Please reassure me that this is the right course of action, I'm being driven unknowing and I'd never want to impose on you or anything like that.

This is so startling!

Lots of love,

Carol

November 16, 1974

Dear Carol,

I am electrified. First by the message in your letter, then by the prospect of seeing you here. We are so alike: First I thought: I must go to

Edmonton. Then later I thought: And make her so disappointed, perhaps, when she sees me? Then, much better, I thought, let this be the ideal relationship where you live in reality and not in the limitations of physical illusions? Let us never see each other in the flesh. But if you say, we are, and reap whatever consequences.

I don't know why I say it, but you may have concluded from my writing about my daughter that, from the records I am old enough to have a daughter (and I have a son too) and, like you having Gary, I have Evelyn, to whom I am married and who will be so happy to see you. And, while we both have friends, we try to not do anything that might hurt the other. For the moment you and I are in heaven together. How will it be when we meet? In a wilder more exciting heaven?

Yes, you will be taken care of, free of all expense, during the three or more days you say you can stay here. Our home is too small but we have some acceptable facilities outside, near here. If you take the ferry to Bremerton and phone 692-2997 from there I shall come and pick you up. How will I know you? Be sure to phone me before you set out, since I am in the course of changing job from Washington to California. Yes, I work weekdays but not Saturdays and can also take a day or two off if I know in advance.

If after what I told you above, you still wish to come, Oh, would I be pleased, and if you don't come I will still love you, mysteriously, sadly, happily, rocking with the waves.

Oh Carol!

Shamcher

November 22, 1974

Oh Dearest Shamcher,

Why is it that when I am away from you there is so much I want to tell you yet when I am with you I have nothing at all to say? I suppose you will be tired of me by now, yet here is something which I must write....

I am now at the airport, waiting to go and feeling inside like: "I must write to him."

Thank you so much for all that you are and for your kind patience with me. How could I express to you the depth of this feeling? (Especially since I can hardly fathom it myself?)

On the bus going away from you I had many regrets. Was I often impolite, just accepting all you gave me as if it were a "given," without truly expressing my gratitude? Oh, what can I do for you? How can I express this love? It is embarrassing to me to be crying here in the airport - those tears I was stuffing back down inside myself Sunday and Monday have all come out now, and it never seems to stop.

Do thank Evelyn for me, for accepting me into her home and her life, and for sharing herself with me, for the food and conversation.

Now when I move, I feel in the movement that it is something that you might do. And when I speak, I sometimes feel it's something that could as easily have come from your mouth. And yet we are very different, but in this difference we come together and can love each other.

Truly, it is you who have opened my heart, and I feel it opens to encompass even your vastness - though I can't possibly understand or express this feeling. And how presumptuous of me to say I can contain you - we share, both of us, in this wonder. How grateful I am to have met you and forever I will love you because I am yours.

Please understand that these words are too clumsy - see it this way too: I breathe in and I breathe you into me. I breathe out and go into you. You breathe me in and we both circle and flow through these frail bodies forever.

I've had enough of this puzzle - this figuring out and wording it. I can't imagine travelling to see you again until the summer, when we could come by car. But perhaps. Oh I am sure, we will be together person to person before then, for I love you so.

How could you ever think I would be disappointed? These tears have nothing at all to do with sadness. They just come through the body when I feel so deeply for you/with you/in you/through you. Consider this letter to be a gentle kiss through the air. And please forgive me for any small error or foolishness I may have shown to you.

Love,
Carol

November 29, 1974

Dear Carol,

Your letter from the airport - as beautiful as your whole visit. So beautiful and so complete that - what is there more to say? We talked out all and everything or, what we didn't talk out we felt out and thought out.

Evelyn was as happy with your visit. What more fine person to

19

entertain and entertaining is her life. I brought her your message. She loved it.

Write, please, whenever you feel like it, whether you have anything to say or not. A word. Two words.

Our son came home, found the whole community buzzing: Who was that girl, visiting with your parents? Silverdale, a small town.
Love,
Bryn, Shamcher

December 3, 1974

Dear Shamcher,

I had thought that perhaps the visit to you would cure me of this intense feeling (not that I would ever want it to go) but I have found that it has all just remained; not increased but deepened. I wish to write you a million words! Not just one or two, but a million! But the more I write doesn't mean the more I express, yet there is such a peace in sending these thoughts to you. And any note, any word I receive from you I greatly value as an expression of your being - that being of you with whom I feel so connected.

I feel like a fountain just pouring it out to you continuously. Any chance to express this to you is to me a great joy. Thank you for allowing me to write to you in this way - I had a little shyness, feeling that pages and pages could somehow overburden you with all these words, but I am so sure that your understanding of me is clear that I go ahead anyways, and will write to you forever, in words and in thoughts and always.

When I came back home, it was so good to be with Gary. He felt as I did that it was the best thing I could have done to go to you. The enclosed writing will tell you a little of what happened to me on a visit to old friends this past weekend. Please if you could tell me what your interpretation of the whole thing is, I would appreciate any help you can give me in this area.

Another thing which has happened to me since knowing you (this began with the first letters) is that I can't seem to get to work. I spend my days at home with the phone off the hook, doing the exercise you showed me or reading Inayat Khan or writing poems. It's all I can do.

I have a poem which was written on my return home. When we first met, I spoke to you of this thought, and it has been obsessing my mind ever since.

20

Here it is:

WISHGIFT

You are old, I am young;
Come into my body when you die, our souls will truly co-operate.
Come into this body when you die, I offer this self to you
To carry on your work.
Come into this body when you die, we'll truly share this life
 together
And even if you must go on
To other realms beyond the sun,
You'll still be in my body when you die,
For forever our souls are one.

Hello to you is all this letter really says - take care, remember that I'm part of you, I think of you and care for you always.

This desire to just suspend my life to have it totally absorbed in you...I mean you the man you the god you the angel you the everybeing you the everything the Bryn the Shamcher - what eyes you have!

Carol

P.S. I know, though I wish to give all to you, this is a part of my discovery of my true self. I was for a time confused, or perhaps it just wasn't clear; I don't think I ever wanted to become you, but to join with you (as we are in essence One.) So I felt the need to clarify to you my understanding of this and to share with you the full fruition of this thought: that I give all to you and share all with you as myself, for I know that my path is my own and my being, if it were covered over in yours, it would not then be my own fulfillment. And, as myself, I love you - yourself; in this way we share being. It's so inexpressible, complex, deep, simple, natural, this loving - I'm a fool to try to write it down.

Here's the enclosed journal page:

I have just returned from a visit with old friends. I was forever having to withdraw from being with people and lie down and rest, or somehow find that still place inside of me from which I could return renewed and refreshed to begin again.

Until this visit I hadn't realised just how much I had changed from the time with Shamcher, just how deep that went I still cannot even fathom, but I will resonate the feelings forever.

The difference in perceptions and the difference in me has made me think that despite the lack of formality and actual ritual, there has been some sort of initiation, some sort of transmission which has gone between us. If he says that it was an initiation, then I will feel free to say that, but until he tells me, I can only say thanks to him (God through him) there seems to be a little less of me and a little more of that light of God, that energy beyond my own personal power.

December 5, 1974

Dear Shamcher,

You said to me on Sunday morning when we were together that you wanted to teach me everything you had learned from your teacher - oh, please, please, will you?

Already from the subtle effect of the morning exercises and the often powerful effects of the zikar I feel encouraged to carry on in this way. Several thoughts are all in a jumble - I want to actually realize God in my being - always, not only in glimpses. Although I feel it is sort of unnecessary to state this in such flat terms, I want to express this to you.

Yes, it is all gradual and perhaps I need to learn patience as the only lesson, but I also know that you could (as you do already) guide me through much of this. I can make wrong choices, and don't wish to get lost, so maps and a guide are what I now need.

I also wonder if approaching you in this manner is incorrect, I'm not sure of the procedure so I'm just asking you: is there a way I could learn through you? Please understand that I realize that I must go alone, I think now I have gone through the total leaning-on-you phase, I want only to purify myself entirely of "me" to fully express God always, to always consciously be aware and in control. Then I want to teach others to do the same. I want us all to be joyful in that peace. But I don't want to get lost or waste precious time following blind alleys.

You are helping me immensely in this now and perhaps it is presumptuous of me to ask for more, especially when I don't know exactly what it is I'm asking for. Something I have been wondering about, which has made me hesitant, is that you always have said I should go here or there or somewhere else, always sending me elsewhere. If you do that with me now, I will accept it but will not understand it, for you are the one for me, that's all I can say.

Can I come to see you after Christmastime, and stay for a week and learn from you and love you in person instead of from a distance? Is this too much to ask? I feel like such a child, wondering if I am somehow stepping over some bounds, but I must follow what I feel is right.

Love,

Carol

P.S. This letter frightens me just a little, almost enough to stop me from sending it to you. Actually, if things were happening any faster, these changes through me, I wouldn't be able to keep up with them at all - then where would I be? So I say, come on, wonders, clean me out!

December 7, 1974

Dear Shamcher,

I was oh-so-expecting a letter from you today, and when none arrived, I decided that it would be better to write to you than to fret around.

Whatever the reason, the feelings are of sadness and a little regret for the errors I keep making. All I see are all my selfish faults and my laziness. I know I'll work it through. It's so much like having a baby - one big push and then a backward force, then another forward with another backward. It's gradually birthing, and the baby is ME! Now I'm at a time of seemingly going backwards.

The other night doing the zikar I became afraid. I totally trust this, so why should I feel fear? It's since then that I've been brought back to earth. THUD!

You know I think of you often; fondly and passionately, kindly and amazed. Thank you for putting up with this particular state of mind. Even in the sad times, I must remain aware so I can see where I'm just expressing the sadness and where I'm getting stuck in self-pity.

Why do I write you all these things?

The mailman came and left without any word from you, so I will mail this anyways.

I am still afraid, though not as afraid as yesterday. I know I have no choice, and I trust in God. There is a feeling that all this will go soon; a glimmer of something tells me that soon all this will go and then where will I be? Am I making any sense to you at all? I hardly understand myself any more, but just keep going, trying to let go of what I am hanging on to, just paying attention to when it's time to let go. Letting go of the feelings, letting go of the anxieties, letting go of each moment as it is.

23

Tomorrow I go to a meeting for the conference I am coordinating and I will tell them that I can no longer do it. Someone else will have to take it over. If no one can, then I will still do it, but if there is anyone else who has an interest in it, they can do it. My whole sense of priorities has gone upside down (or else has always been until now) and I cannot put my energy into that conference which is just politics. Better to spend my time in other areas, especially now.

I love you dearly, as you know, and how I hope to hear from you soon. Of course, with Christmas coming, I imagine that communication by letter will become more and more difficult. Can you tell me why I feel so abandoned and empty and alone? Or do I have to work this one out, like all the rest of this journey, on my own? I wish 1 were with you now, beside you. I don't seem to have any questions then.

Love,

Carol

December 9, 1974

Dear Carol,

From your envelope from the airport I fished out your letter only, and days later when I was to discard the envelope I found the beautiful and significant mandala, copy of which is enclosed, with a rent heart, and, as my teacher Inayat said, "When my heart had been crushed a thousand times, I began to see my soul." And I enclose vague copies of the other beautiful mandalas. They show, apart from insight in symbols, great patience and endurance seeing and expressing the winding ways and paths of spiritual probes and realization.

Your Tuesday and Thursday letters: with the poems, that are showing your depth and understanding in love. You are unequalled among the ones who have come to me. That does not mean these others are "lower" than you. They are tops, in their genre - and so are you, miles ahead of the "teachers" in Vancouver and Victoria. And I did not tell you to see others because I preferred you to go there, but I wanted you to see them and make a choice. For I am somewhat different in my approach: I do not initiate formally. If I should, you would be so high up the bishops in San Francisco would scream and holler. I did once initiate a girl into a certain grade because she asked for it. All kinds of havoc happened.

I will only tell you this: You are entitled now, today, to teach Sufism

24

as I taught you to any and all in Canada. And I am very happy this will be through you and not by other channels. For you have the finesse to realize that formal initiations into fixed degrees are no more the thing. Do as I do, initiate silently in your heart and find out if they understand. Then you never boast to anyone you have a certain degree - nor do you grovel before one who says he has one. And I will help you with letters and thoughts and Yung Lee visits (haven't you felt them already???) And real visits, but perhaps not yet January.

When Inayat Khan left for India and his last year, he had reached the same concept that I now have. And one of his sons, Hidayat, a wonderful musician, agrees. Pir Vilayat feels as yet he has to be true to Inayat's earlier methods with definite initiations stages. Nevertheless, in 1970 at a large meet in Los Angeles Pir Vilayat suddenly said, "We have with us here tonight the esoteric (inner) head of the Sufi Order, Shamcher, who now will address us." I did address them though taken by surprise, Later I said, "That was nice of you to say, Pir Vilayat, but now please release me again from this strange and august position." "I cannot, Shamcher, for it was not me who elevated you, it was my father."

So even formally I am entitled to do and say what I did and said to you. And if you are worldly wise you may "make money" or make it pay to establish the Sufi Order through Shamcher, in Canada. Your Gary may help. I never could make it pay but you may. You are deeper, more whole in heart than I was at your age. The few exercises you have already are enough for the required, or with no more at all if the pupil is really good. It is not the exercises who make the pupil. They correct him when correction is due. It is the heart that makes him, her.

After I joined my teacher I marched into other professions until I became a generalist, knowing more about money, psychology, than my original subject of engineering, being chosen by our prime minister to restore Norway's economy after WW II crush, being sent by the United Nations to Tunisia, head of economic mission... but protect yourself against depletion by simply asking for and consciously accepting protection from GOD in your heart.

Love,

Bryn, Shamcher

December 13, 1974

Dear Shamcher,

Thank you for your letter - stating the things I had felt but really dared not to think. I don't know how to respond to this but to say thank you -I feel in a sense that you see me in the future, for at this time I feel so clouded over and unworthy. Yet I do know in my heart.

Usually when I write to you the words just pour out, but this letter is slow and different. I almost wish to start writing again, and I have read and reread your letter to me for many days before even sitting down to write back to you. Part of my hesitance is regret, or foolish-feeling, for the last letter I sent. The strength behind your last letter - all I can say is: I've felt all that you told me in that letter and to have you state that reinforces my trust in the unworded intuitions, reinforces my strength to persevere and keep always God in my heart, the thought of God in my heart.

I'm not giving up my job with that conference. Through many circumstances and events I learned that I needn't do that, so I'll be diving into it. Just your words "guard against depletion" were a great help to me. I had been afraid of that, I think, and that is why I spent all my time away from the pressures of the world. But with perseverance and constant attention, with awareness of God in my heart, and in others and in all, I think I can make it - and certainly this is the main work.

Please, please excuse my foolishness of the last letter. I was asking you to write me more often, making demands of you in a sense, when all I really want to do is just love you, love God through you and actually love myself through this whole process. I just want to find out who I am and be it! I see now that this is the only way to be close to you, because what is you is also me. Nothing would give me greater peace than to be with you - together in all planes at once resonating through one another that feeling which draws me to you always.

I know this love is deepening despite the physical separation. The implications and power of our union are such that I dare not think at all. I accept all that you so powerfully told me in that letter, and will work to clear myself out so I can do what must be done in its perfection, the best that is possible through me. What else can be said? Only thank you, I love you, you are always in my being.

Love,

Carol

P.S. I've been thinking of this Sufism as a moment to moment or day to day change. When you wrote that the exercises I now do are good for the first three years I was deeply struck! I hadn't even thought of three years from now - amazement!!

Inside a birthday card is typed:

December 19, 1974

Dear Carol,

Your last letter looks like you did not receive my two letters - one after your airport letter and the next with copies of your beautiful mandalas. And your letter was torn.

Please, please answer at once whether you got my two previous letters or not. *(No you needn't. We just phoned. It as lovely.)*

There is a meet - in San Anselmo, would you like to come? If you want to go, please write and tell them that I have invited you and that I consider it urgent that you are admitted. First, however, write and tell me if you received my two previous letters.

(Not necessary any more, dear Carol, I phoned after writing.)

Love,

Shamcher

HAVE A VERY, VERY HAPPY BIRTHDAY!

December 17, 1974

Dear Shamcher,

I now feel very much like writing to you - friend, lover, father, son, teacher, pupil, everybody, me. I have felt so close to you in these past days, and I'm a little stronger, too.

Everyone is preparing for Christmastime here, and my thoughts often turn to Cory. He was always so excited and had such fun at Christmas. How different it will be for us this year! Halloween was also hard because every child who came to the door in anticipation would remind me of my son, the Halloweener, in disguise. This Christmas will be sad, but also warm and good, for what is shared between us in friendship and relation is the same as what was shared with Cory. I still will feel his presence/absence and will no doubt feel as deeply as I do at this moment. Once I was particularly sad and there was a poem which came. The main thought in it was that what I feel here on earth is loss, but I must transmute that and send it to him as love and a

27

godspeed on his way. Even now I wish him goodnight each night as if I were still tucking him in. But when I feel the loss of his sweet nature, it always comes through very hard, with a good deal of crying and tenderness. I don't cry for him, you know, I cry for me.

You suggested I read *The Soul Whence and Whither*, and I've been reading it - how wonderful! I've imagined it as a beautiful animated film (what a wonderful project that would be!) and I find it provides a workable frame of reference. At this point, of course, I believe it totally but have yet to experience it consciously - though poems have hinted the exact-same world. It is helpful.

In years past I became more and more disillusioned with Christmas. It seemed that Christmas had become its opposite, to bring out the lowest aspects of people. Now more and more I see it differently. The lights on the houses remind me of the bright light of the spirit, a reminder of the birth of the spirit in us all. If, even unconsciously, we are reminding each other of that brightness and goodness then Christmas fulfills its purpose. But if we were all conscious of it, the celebration would have greater effect.

You know, without me telling you, how deeply I feel your presence. This letter is just extra, unnecessary decoration. I send it to you anyways, because I love you here on earth as well.

Take care - be well - I love you
Carol

December 22, 1974

Carol ....

Your messages, particularly in your last two letters, roll on in majestic melodious rhythms, touching truth and my soul. And to keep my physical being and passion in high gear you even paint the tantalizing figures of ecstatic angels and hindu saints, in all of which I see you, you and again you. Not only sublime wisdom, but touched by sublime excitement. Thank you. Thank you.

Sufis are seekers after truth, whether they call themselves Sufis or not. A Sufi is accepted as such as soon as he wants to call himself so, or even if he won't. To me, everyone in the whole wide world may be called a Sufi, or, if not, then I may not be one either. A Sufi may know all the jokes and tricks of a magician but he is more serious than any saint or government economist or garbage collector. And he loves them all with a love so fierce, so bitter, and so sweet that in comparison with this love, the magnitude of it, he himself disappears, and no longer exists.

Carol, my breath is you and you are my breath.

Love,
Shamcher

Undated

Carol, Dear Carol,

What do you think you did to me with that new mandala and the doodling numbered one to eleven? I cannot describe it. I am dizzy, dizzy with joy, with happiness and excitement and you are here, around and in me!
Shamcher

Undated

Dear Carol,

Oh, with you it is so much much more than just "dear carol" so the dear seems so flat, undescribing. For you tread this earth with a magic touch, discernable even in letters written from a thousand miles away.

Your offer of driving our Chrysler down to SF seemed at first delightful. It is 700 miles, would probably require staying over once on the road, but worse: Last time we, Bryn, Daphne and myself drove that way at this time of year, over the mountains in Northern California, a snow storm took us by surprise. We could not even see the road. We had no time to put on chains. It is just a benevolent fluke of God the (supposedly) almighty which made us survive and continue living on this side of death. We had to backtrack to find what we thought was a motel and, by golly, found it and knocked on the door. "Oh, no," they shook their heads, "We cannot take you, we have no television!" How we laughed, and then took possession of a huge apartment of five rooms, all for $12 - at Weed, in the California mountains.

Carol, precious dear Carol, I could not expose you, of all people, all women, to such risk. I couldn't, however much I'd love to. But if you happened to be at the Seattle airport Friday 17, just before 5, or say 4:30, then with my magic American express card we could buy two plane tickets to SF and the same back to Seattle on Tuesday or Wednesday, you then going on to Edmonton (or by another route?) and I staying in Seattle.

Before you make up your mind, I must confess something with a heavy heart, heavy because it might change your mind about coming with me to SF: Pir Vilayat is giving a talk in Seattle 25 February this year. So you could see and talk to him with much less waste of time and expense than coming to SF, though of course you would see much more of him, and hear and talk much more with him by coming to the seminar at SF. But it is my duty to place all these alternatives before you, so you can make a wise choice.

Oh, Carol, your wonderful letters make me tremble and shoot out of myself, what are you doing to me? And when you write about your shortcomings and such I must laugh. You, shortcomings? Ah, I am so curious, tell me all about them, perhaps I would feel they were additional wonderful excitements about you.

Carol, I could not possibly ask you to come to this dull trip to SF but if you would...

Love

Bryn

You'd have to order this Western flight No. 635 if you want to do that, order it from Edmonton. If I have a cold or something I won't come, won't communicate it to the crowd at SF, nor should anyone else if they have a cold I feel. But who?

1975
LOVE'S LABYRINTH

You know your feeling of being lost, of no longer knowing yourself is just a sign of welcome development. For actually, you don't exist. The prevalent idea that each person is a separate unit, a so-and-so, different from and separated from anyone else is just an illusion. All minds are connected with the Universal Mind and interconnected, and when you begin to realize this it is at first confusing. "Who am I? Where am I?" You are in everybody.

Shamcher

January 2, 1975

Dear Shamcher,

How wonderful to receive two letters from you today, and once again they told me just what I needed to be reminded of! Just on this day when it seems some wave within has broken - some built-up pretense shifting away and falling down - then your sweet letters!

It seems like waves and waves of different experiences are just roaring through. When I block it, then it becomes difficult. If I let it pass then it just passes. As soon as I experience what's going on - always a little lag between the knowing and the experiencing.

More and more it just doesn't seem to matter. Oh yes! I wish to express all the sorrows and joys - to be all that is, purely and joyfully. I can think this, but will it happen? I am hanging on to whatever shreds of what-I-think-is-real I can lay my hands on, but the shreds are fewer all the time. What I used to consider my greatest tool - my mind and thinking ability, I now see as my greatest impediment - and it is both.

Today I visited my mother, who is sick. On the way home I cried and cried for all the things that have passed, for all the feelings and for all the years - it came in waves. Just when I'd feel all cried out, more would come. I so wanted to somehow express this feeling, whatever it is, in a fine form. After the crying, part of me was open again. All this: waves of feeling, crying and laughing, being open and then finding myself closed up again - again the waves of feeling and crying and opening all over again.

I came home after such a time to your two good letters, and your strong presence. You are such a help to me! I can't say thank you enough.

Lots of love forever and kisses in all that you are near - trees, air, chair, etc. I send you a greeting of kisses and love through the air, the ground, and bouncing off the stars.

Love,
Carol

January 28, 1975

Dear Carol,

It was a long week, no word from you...and then it came - pages and pages of beautiful music, rhythm and joy, bundled up in an appearance of humility and reticence. Every word you write is you, the whole of your beautiful self, adorable. Now you know about such a seminar. There are two approaches: "This is above my head, too far up in the sky, gave me nothing really," and then they are not benefiting much. Then there is the other attitude: "Oh, what precious beauty, so much I didn't know, I feel so small, so grateful" - well that is you, and it shows that you are all there, fully realized, aware of all there was, just being reminded. For the words are not the reality, only a sign, a jolt, a reminder to those who already have the reality, which you have. A vision, which words may awake to life.

Please tell me all about when you came back, what happened, what mood your friends and loved ones were in. And tell me, please, about those days in San Anselmo when I was not there under the warmth of your glowing, loving *sun*.

If you only knew, Carol, what has happened to me because of you, you, you.
Love,
Bryn, Shamcher, 07

L O V E

February 4, 1975

Carol,

Your letters are so much you that they sing and dance and make me sing too, and tremble. And your name Carol is so yours that I couldn't think of any Sufi name that would be better. Besides, as you say, friends already seemed somewhat remote to you when you returned, and how much more remote would they become if you trooped up with a new name too? I find it most natural that they seem remote and a bit hurt that you leave for a whole week after having left for days only a couple of months before. Besides, they are not yet part of that special wine the Sufis ooze out, of love, LOVE for all and everybody. How could they be?

So I am reluctant to see you leave them again. So although I pine and hurt and go crazy not to be with you all the time, how can I ask you to come? I can't. Maybe we shall never be together again? Or will we? If you say come, I cannot say no. For ... you know. But if you nevertheless want a Sufi name, ask Pir Vilayat. The Norwegian leader Susanna Kjoesterud never was given a Sufi name. Inayat Khan said her name was good enough.

Carol, you are the perfect thing, perfect in my world, belonging in it forever, and all your friends belong in it too. That's what makes it so difficult, or perhaps not difficult, only challenging, interesting. What do we do? What

33

do we not do? I cannot help loving you, desperately, completely.

Yours,

Shamcher (The Sword of the Message, The Tongue of Flame - said Inayat Khan)

Feb 11, 1975

Carol,

Essence of your letters pierced my heart, from there ascended to my head and then flowed out under and around my eyes, along the upper part of my mouth, through the solar and lunar nostrils and made my breath fragrant and buoyant. What have you done to me? You have made me new and pure, you have made me one with you and all.

Outside of us is a world that has to be treated with care and respect, and not quite openly. For the openness is not understood.

I am enjoying both the joy and blessing and pain you cause me. The pain, of course, is really caused by myself.

A simple word, but so great: LOVE.

Shamcher

February 18, 1975

Dear Carol,

Hello. Letter from you today, and tales of other letters you didn't send. Why? I want to see them all, you know. I want to follow your mind on paper just as in spirit.

You know your feeling of being lost, of no longer knowing yourself is just a sign of welcome development. For actually, you don't exist. The prevalent idea that each person is a separate unit, a so-and-so, different from and separated from anyone else is just an illusion. All minds are connected with the Universal Mind and interconnected, and when you begin to realize this it is at first confusing. "Who am I? Where am I?" You are in everybody. That's why many want to belong to a good friend or teacher at this time, for it is easier to see the connection with such a being than with anybody. And it is a safer way. But congratulate yourself that you don't quite "find" yourself now. Who do you think I am? Nobody and everybody. But is this good? Yes, excellent, and besides: it is true. Truth is better than falsehood, even though falsehoods are sometimes comfortable to some - for a while at least.

I have no ambition of being "somebody" anymore. I enjoy being a hammock swinging with the punches, with the neighboring minds. The more ardent you keep at it, the better and greater are the minds you contact and swing with. You may even become impressed, and fascinated.

Carol, I love you and I hope to always feel your wishes and desires right.
Shamcher

February 21, 1975

Dear Carol,

The words Pir Vilayat gave you were *Ya Shaffee Ya Kaffee*, old Arab, providing physical and all-round health, healing. Did you tell him what practices you had already?

Yes, I am the bad boy of the Sufi effort to some, and the good boy to others, because I accept nothing that isn't already in me. I see that stagewise gradual development through an accepted "teacher" can be all right for some cases, and also can lead the aspirant to stand pat and never go forward or even backward. Anyway, it is not *my* way, neither as a "pupil" or a "teacher". The only thing I can do is to live and act myself all the time, and those who like it, fine, and those who don't, equally fine. For who am I (or anyone else??) to judge whether a seeker shall have only a nickel or a whole dollar or all of yourself? The least you can give is all of yourself, at once and forever. And he or she who feels like a pupil today, why should he (she) not switch to a teacher, away from his once-upon-a-time teacher the next second? Indeed, he ought to. Pir Vilayat has shown great understanding and perhaps agreement, though he naturally must and does act differently.

In the same vein, who am I (or anyone) to "initiate" another person? Well, say the pious, it isn't you but God who initiates him. Well, don't you think God can do that without my help? I am sure he can. Personally I see no virtue or advantage in the ritual of initiation. But if you want it, take it. A friend who visited me said, "I want to have all I can of Sufi teachings but don't initiate me, for that would separate me from others, from parents, wife, and friends who are not initiated." I said: "You are perfectly right." Nevertheless, in New York he was now initiated. I was initiated myself, by Inayat Khan. I have no objection, nor any inclination. I can initiate you in a higher degree so you can initiate others. Just to follow the rules. Actually, whenever my glance strikes another human being, or a tree, a dog, it, she,

35

he, is initiated by me and I by him, her, it, in a whole lot holier unity than any formal words or sign. And all this appears to be accepted heartily by Pir Vilayat, by his father Inayat Khan (who left his body in 1927) and especially by Inayat Khan's musician son, Hidayat.

The Sufi effort needs many kinds of people, also my kind. Though I am ready to jump out any time I am pushed. I will be the same. I don't recommend, suggest or discommend initiations. I asked you to come to San Anselmo and meet and see Sufis whom you had shown interest in, among them Pir Vilayat, and he initiated you as you so wished. Physically it entitles you to certain accesses. I can give you an initiation that entitles you to initiate Gary or any of your friends.

No wonder your girl friend is afraid of me, representing big clumsy USA gobbling up Canadian businesses. She does not know that I actually come from the humblest smallest Norway, whose settlers in this territory 600 years ago married and befriended the Indians and never would have treated them the way they were treated, nor would have tried to gobble up Canada. And if you talk to her about me the way you talk to me about me, of course she must be frightened.

Yes, Carol, there are only the two of us in all the world, and not even that, there is only one, and that one is us. So of course I am as desperate to see you as it is possible to be, but I wonder, is it right? And tell me some time what you thought it all would be, San Anselmo would be, I would be, and how we became so different, so confusing to you, so upsetting. Is it because you expected to reach a firm concept, know it all, and found you know less and less? But that is excellent, the exactly right direction. All "knowledge" will drop from your mind like useless toys, and you will begin to see but not with your mind though.
Love,
Shamcher

March 4, 1975
The waves go up and down, sometimes my little boat is soaring, sometimes it is almost drawn under.
I must leave this boat and walk upon the waters direct.
Oh, Shamcher,

It seems I'm in another spell as deep and powerful as when we were first in contact. Before I had met you and knew you only through letters, I was caught in such a spell - not knowing what I was saying, driven to see you by physical things - my body just sick and sighing. And now here I am again - in a similar state. What is this? All sorts of thoughts go through me and many are so encoded and cryptic that they make no sense at all. I know that whatever this profound upheaval is will be clear later on.

Whatever it is that I must get rid of now is a big one because it's causing a tremendous physical and emotional upheaval. Yet it's not just that some part of me is hanging on, it's also pulling and driving me to the new part, the wide-open me. It could be that this is it - I'm actually in the process of dying. What I'm hanging on to is me! Sometimes, when I'm afraid of too big of a change, the wildness and anguish set in. But it's all within, I just have to balance this rhythm - so that inner and outer and up and down I am unified and not scrambled. For this to work, the unsettled aspects must be smoothed or destroyed. I cannot go back and I'm afraid to go forward. But since I'm impelled and compelled to go forward no matter what, then I will dive in wholeheartedly and rush on with the forward wave, leaving the shell of my former self far behind.

The question is - if I feel yes, great universal Zond, take me, I'm totally yours - I no longer exist - only You - what then? The question is how? I keep asking and I sincerely mean it because there's a lot here to keep me here, yet I'd go totally away, give it all, all up - everything, everyone, even me. I would dive in and give up. Yet even this saying it isn't it, this is just circling the main vortex which is black hole of space (seen from here) but within I feel such a love and a longing I know it's all I want and all that can be and all is nothing without this one thing and I'll give away my whole self to you lord - open me so you can play through me.
Love,
Carol

March 11, 1975

Dear Carol,

Here is a copy of a letter to Hidayat. If I can believe him, I am his closest friend and certainly he is mine. I know that a big company had taken over his tapes and I do not know if he can do as I ask; but if he can he will.
Fond greetings,
Shamcher

March 11, 1975

My dear precious Pir-Hidayat,

I have this musician friend whose wife has visited me repeatedly. These are two special kinds of musicians, who have read and reread your father's works, particularly on music. She is a Sufi initiate and may initiate her husband. He is a performer particularly yearning for new and spiritual music. He is now a teacher of many aspects of music, and though the humblest of men, he may become a great light some day.

They both want so very much to have some of your music and I would think of such as your stunning music about your sister, your zikar piece, and your Ghandi piece, any one of them, preferably the first.

Is there any chance that you could send them one or two of your tapes? With any restriction you might want to impose upon them. They would accept it as securely as I would.

I know that the enclosed cheque does not begin to pay for your incomparable music, it is only intended to cover expenses. Some day, I am confident, I shall be able to pay a fraction of what I owe you for having had the priceless privilege of hearing and absorbing your music.
In admiration and devotion,
Shamcher

March 13, 1975

Dear Shamcher,

I received your letter today, the one with the copy of your letter to Hidayat. That was so kind of you to ask him for us. And your letter itself was so wonderfully loving and gentle - truly you amaze me all the time. You turn and there you are with an entirely new aspect, then you turn again, and another side shines and shines. And this goes on forever.

I feel so limited, selfish and ungainly beside you. This is beside you as we are at this moment - for your being extends here to me right now. So much to learn - I'm like a baby learning to walk, knocking things over, sometimes destroying that which is precious by this grasping curiosity. Here in this land of the heart I'm so clumsy and new. But I know that as this terrain becomes familiar, new wonders will open again and again and forever I'll be just beginning.

There are times when I think matter-of-factly of you. Times when I think kindly of you. Times when I care for you with concern. Times when

I absolutely need to be with you. Times when I'm happy just to know you. Times when I feel you with me. Times when I'm so sad to be apart from you. Times when I think you could not possibly care for me. Times when I love you so deeply I cry and cry. Times when the thought of you helps me and heals me. Lots of other times all happening at once, it just depends on which comes forward, on how open I am. It's like this: I see you so many-faceted, and our relationship is many-faceted. A crystal jewel we share and create and live within.

Love,

Carol

Waves and waves of love through me to you! Folding this letter, I remembered standing outside in the dark with you, with our foreheads together - so still and so deep.

March 15, 1975

Dearest Shamcher,

Why does everything change so fast? Why am I always tricked into thinking that I know what is going on?

Every day since I've been home from the visit, I've cried and cried. So much is happening, there seems so much to cope with. I just let go and do what I can. Then I find I'm still holding on somewhere, to some set idea of what is real, and when that is blasted open I feel free and unafraid and peaceful, not really concerned with the so-called "problems" I used to think were so terrifying and important.

Though I see all the traits that hold me back, I look forward, too, feeling hopeful and confident. It helps to know that you are here as a friend and helper in this changing - I suppose I rely on you more than you know and yet also on myself - (you are myself deep inside.)

I can say again - what have you done to me? Or I can say thank you or I can say I love you or I can just be as I am with you inside me always. And I am inside you, too, kissing you from the inside, and outside in the air, too.

Love,

Carol

March 21, 1975

Dear Carol,

You leave, with a ferry, and then after a few days you come back, as much alive, as true, or more, as in your body... in your letter. You were given the gift of presenting yourself, wide awake and beautiful in the hieroglyphs or letters chained together on a sheet of paper - for anyone who can read, at least.

Not only do your letters speak to my mind, but they also speak and shout and whisper and sigh to my heart. And my soul.

"You are vast," you say. But as they say in Norway, "It takes one to know one." Every human being and also every tree is vast. And she who sees that vastness is vast herself. It is in her vastness that she sees another's.

Pir Vilayat is here tomorrow. They have asked me to introduce him, and I like nothing better, for in those few words I can say a lot I wouldn't be able to say otherwise. But I have asked the ones who ask me to first ask Pir Vilayat if he really wants to be introduced by me. Of course, I have done it often before. But one never knows when a person changes his mind about whom he wants to be introduced by. Lord Northcliffe once listened to a man taking such a long time introducing him that, when finally that introducing gentleman ended by saying, "And now Lord Northcliffe will give us his address ..."

The good lord rose and answered, "Yes, my address is 33 Picadilly Circus," and sat down. He thought enough had been said that evening.

Carol, know your potentiality, your vastness, which is really yours, not necessarily mine. And use your unimaginable young power to conquer and own all that you wish to conquer and own. And please never let anyone come too close, but preserve your sanctuaries for the ones your inner lord and master has so ordained. Countless treasures, sentiments, land, gold, silver and rubies are floating in your aura, eager to serve you, to be taken possession of, to serve any wider purpose you may conceive.

There comes a time for some, when no diet is necessary; the mind, the soul, masters the body at whatever diet or no diet is accepted. But generally people should not fool themselves and imagine they are on that stage.
LOVE,
Shamcher

40

March 22, 1975

Dear Shamcher,

As I look on the times and the changes since I have known you, it is impossible to feel as I did before knowing you. Now is all I am and you truly have given me this tiny glimpse of myself (that shines way down at the end of a dark tunnel.) I wonder now, just where is it that you really dwell? I know you work, you live in your house, but where do you really dwell? I wish you were here with me now and that we could look at one another and melt into one another forever.

Life is beautiful to me, all is singing, you are within me always and our love is a precious thing to me - which is deeper and truer than anything I've ever known. And certainly l can say that I can't ever know just what this is, or how far it reaches, or the reasons and implications, for all I can tell is that we are together as the true one which we are in this place of our love (which is not ours because in this place who are we?)

I love you dearly and hope to hear from you very soon.

Love,

Carol

March 26, 1975

Dear Carol,

First part of your last letter seemed a little angry because you didn't know where or what you were. What builds the wings on the butterfly, and what does the butterfly think about it? Man was supplied with reason to be able to follow the beautiful creative process. Instead, man has leaned on reason, believing it something else than it is.

If there is anything in religion, yoga, Sufism or whatever, it is to free man again from this illusion, and never try the idiotic experiment trying to understand what, who he is or if he makes "progress". In the beginning this unlearning is painful if it is not understood. You are right that I never look back to judge or learn. I look back sometimes to see what I did which would have turned out so differently if I had the insight then.

What happens after a while of understanding the limitation of reasoning is that you get insight. But not before you have thoroughly rejected reasoning or any effort to "see" where you stand, what you are, or who. That is why the saints say, "I do not exist." We don't. Really. So why worry about our status? Progress? Whatnot? But to the man not seeking, this sounds

41

crazy. So don't try to explain this to outsiders; they may put you in a mental institution.

Yes, it is all right that you phone now and then, but I am in a place where I may be a mile away from my office any time. Our private phone has been out of order for a week. It rings, but no conversation can be heard.

Carol, please don't think that you can "know yourself," please be patient and look with appreciation at life around you. That is you.
I love you,
Shamcher

March 27, 1975

Dear lovely Carol,

More lovely letters from you. May I start with your dream, which came last? Dreams are almost always revelations from your own subconscious and sometimes superconscious and almost never something that has happened or will happen. The fear of someone reading your letters and ridiculing them has occurred to your subconscious and reflects in a dream. There may be slight addition from the whimsy thoughts of friends, but nothing to worry about. Your letters are safely kept here, but to still your fears maybe I should burn them? And retain just their flavor in my soul?

The children in the water are on another tack and both together indicate that what you wish to tell yourself is that you might play along with any sentiment you suspect your friends of having, by saying before they have said or even thought about it that, "I am living in the clouds, you know, a thousand leagues above the earth - and your wonderful reality" etc, etc. As I said similarly when giving a concluding talk after Vilayat's speech, "And you know, Sufis still do the most silly things, like this old Dervish in Egypt who walked along throwing all his coins to the children in the street, so some of us do even worse than that: Purport to tell the government and all the geniuses in Congress how we can get out of both depression and inflation and have employment for all, money to throw in the streets, as much as we need..." From cynicism they turn to compassion and goodwill. And I added, "Many envy Vilayat who can travel and sun himself in pupils' devotion but frankly I think I would think twice before I accepted such a job..." Vilayat beside me, laughed and laughed. And if your friends, some of them, insist on scary warnings about my humble person, go along. "Oh, I know, he is the devil himself, otherwise where does he get his money from? I saw him give a guy three whole cents."

Carol, you are wonderful, dreams and all, and don't you forget it.
Clash bang love
Shamcher

April 3, 1975

Dear Carol,

Maybe I'm getting lazy, sending copy of one letter to another instead of spelling it out all over again. Well, I thought some of these answers would interest you, too, although you never asked the same questions. (His: What about all those who claim to be Inayat's only true followers? Why have I pain? Why couldn't the swami cure it when I saw him? Isn't Sufism for the future and yoga of the past? Oh, it wasn't that crowded, a nice letter from him, really.) But I can promise you one thing: I shall never send a copy of a letter to you to somebody else. Unless you ask me to, that is.

Now I have another thing: Would you hate to expand a little on your meditation time: Would you hate to say *Ya Rafa Ya Dafa* after saying all your *Ya Shaffee YaKaffee*? Five or thirty-three times?

Ya Rafa Ya Dafa are old-Arabic words that have been imprinted on the mind world for many thousands of years by strong thinkers. They mean: You jolly playful spirits, not yet in human flesh or perhaps in the past in human flesh; I greet you and love you as you shall now love and help me, and there shall be no cross-purposes in our ways or minds or hearts. We are one, one with the all-embracing Spirit who created and maintained the universes. Co-operate, love and respect. Or about that. As you engrave all that on your being, there will be no more haunting moods, no trouble, no cause for diseases. As *Ya Shaffee Ya Kaffee* brings physical health, so *Ya Rafa Ya Dafa* brings spiritual and even emotional health and good relations with all the ghosts, the advanced ones as well as the not-so-advanced ones. Whenever a mood comes along that seems not too desirable, sing or think *Ya Rafa Ya Dafa* again and again. Any time during the day or night, put it in any melody that suits you, but be sure to retain a definite time morning and evening also. You choose which time you want but keep to it, the same time every morning, in addition to the more accidental times. I set aside 4:40 AM to about 5:40 every morning, except Saturday and Sunday when I do it anytime and then, because unaccustomed, I often go to sleep. So maybe it's wrong of me to do it late on Saturday and Sunday. In the evenings I do it

when I go to bed. I have about ten minutes. Others are the opposite: only a short time in the morning, longer at night. I cannot have it long at night. I am very sleepy then. Fall asleep like a log. Dream about you, lovely Carol.
Shamcher - Bryn - X-15

April 1, 1975

Dear ___

Thank you for good letters to wife and myself. Going back to a previous matter: You are right that specifically the Inayat Khan Sufi effort is typically directed to the future, though this is not so for Sufism in general, except that, like all traditions, it encompasses past-present-and-future. Inayat Khan's "Message" was the future, near and far.

When you come to his "followers", no one really is a follower, however much they try to claim to be an "only" follower - well, the less spoken of the better. But the concept of "following" may be good for a "follower" on a certain stage, and that is all, or it may become bad, if vain and egotistical.

I saw Inayat Khan invest power and appointments in his son Vilayat, who, however, is the first to think and say that he is not his father but himself, trying his best to convey and continue the "Message." Of course, everyone has a message and is worth listening to, sometimes with a laugh, or only a vague smile, and sometimes with interest. But let no one claim to be a "true follower." That is one more reason why discipleship is not always for the best, particularly if the teacher is not supremely developed, and pure and wise.

A special signal is pain. As long as it is accepted as a signal and nothing else, it is good and does its work, fulfills its purpose. If, in addition, it becomes a nuisance or even unacceptable suffering, this is a further signal that one has gone astray, that one has some revision to do. Contact the Creator inside you and outside you, which is really your essential self. Ask "Him" (or her?) why the healthful rays of the universe are not penetrating and completely healing you this very minute, and within seconds or at least hours you should have a reply. The reply may be relief from pain and/or insight into what you should further do for improvement.

No such word has come in regard to you. Indicating that either you will succeed yourself, or you should long ago have applied the medicine recommended. It was your fault that you did not recognize his very unusual

44

development. You could find out in your own way why you didn't.

Anyway, when next time you write, you may have conquered your pain, or know what it tries to tell you.

The path? Well, everyone is on a path, why do you think you are different? Higher? No one is higher. You cannot afford to dwell in your limited concepts ... your experiences looking for that farm were revealing, interesting, and you understood it, just what you got was right, the feeling of unavailability through reason. Reason reaches just so far. Then you have to board another vehicle.

Love,

Shamcher

April 9, 1975

Dear Shamcher,

Your letter with the copy of the other letter was great! Just what I needed to get me back on the track again.

I couldn't possibly digest (absorb, understand, be) all that came in your letter today. I just now received it and had to respond right away. Dear, dear you! Of course I would love to expand my meditation time to include *Ya Rafa Ya Dafa* - it's just what I need, help in clearing the clouds. You know how often I get stuck in false concepts of "what is." I was thinking the other day that such a practice was what I needed. Enough to tell thank you and I will begin with 33 times in the morning and before bed. *Ya Shaffee Ya Kaffee* I do only before bed, should I also practice this in the morning?

Please do not hesitate to give me practices that you feel would be beneficial, thinking that I would hate to do it. This is the most important part of my life (because all my life is this, including and developing and changing in this - I can't express it the way I feel - because the practice alone isn't it either, yet in a sense all that I create/experience in this life is practice.)

Whenever I'm busy or doing a lot with many people, I become easily exhausted. Often if I've been with a group of people for an evening, the next day I need to sleep a lot. And I tend to eat a lot if I am tired in this way. It's not a physical exhaustion, but a mental or spiritual one. Is there anything I can do about this? I shouldn't be so weak, so easily tired.

What a help you are to me! How can I give you all I feel and more? I feel like we are good friends but I am such a child. You must see me as so confused (just as I feel that I know what's happening, that's when I'm most confused.) Yet I feel that I could stand beside you and in your presence be as you are.

Though I feel strong now at this moment, I want very much to be you. Why is this?

Love,

Carol

April 14, 1975

Dear Carol,

Strong, yes, that is you. You see your strength in others, even in me. Thank you. I love you for it, in addition to all the other reasons and no reasons for which I love you. We are using that strength and even our passions to throw ourselves into the spaceways and vitalize the stars and planets.

And now you talk about seeing me again. That raises my emotions to flame in a raging fire of joy - and then comes the second thought: but if this could cause two persons to suffer or possibly suffer, can we still do it? As usual you will have your way through some unforeseen happening, which you probably engineered, for your subconscious and superconscious are so clever. Yes, I would love to see you, but hate to cause suffering to dear ones.

Since you gave the go-ahead with one letter, here is another letter. But no, I could never use your letters (letters to you) thus.

Carol, you speak as if this is just another experience among many with me. Oh no, Carol, this one with you and me has no similar copy anywhere in the universe. It is unique, the only one, and will in time merge into the splendid universe.

Love,

Shamcher, Bryn

April 14, 1975

Dear ___,

We have safely received all books and two letters. The books we hadn't expected back but now we can loan them to others. Your April 4 letter is sweet and interesting. No I did not blame you for bringing up the follower syndrome. I am glad you did. Only: when I answer I have to keep my tongue, not to criticize. That's what I meant by "less spoken of the better." This is only to myself, and to you it shows that I agree with you, that those who think of themselves as "the only true followers" are not clear in their minds

46

or morally. But who is? I am glad you realize it. And you have the information now: Don't be impressed by the "true followers". Except those other assets these "true followers" may possess or temporarily have.

Your remark about your time there makes me realize I was mistaken. Trying to search, I did not know you had been that much involved. On the other hand, after those three days with his environment, you might have established contact, which you seem not to have done. This is a matter of spontaneity. Maybe you reason too long and somewhat ineffectually instead of taking the leap.

In fact: Your reasoning power is highly developed - so highly that you should be ready to discard it in such cases when it should be discarded. This short-coming, that you don't jump into the "other vehicle" (that of intuition) when such is due, is something you share with our entire Western civilization (and today with Eastern civilization too.) All our universities, all sciences, most religion, is 98% working on logic, and reason does not dare leap into the term of intuition.

While this is our most important matter, it is impossible to criticize anybody because from birth to the grave everyone is pushed and forced into the intellectual jail. Yes, it becomes a jail when it no longer applies. So this is not your "fault" but it is something that your contact with a few people who have made the jump may suddenly open your eyes to.

No, your experience of being stopped when looking for a farm does not mean you should not do farming or find a farm. In a sense the contrary. One's soul (which is not often in close contact with the "mind") may deliberately place obstacles in the way to test and increase your strength and determination. Besides, your soul or its agents may stop you from obtaining one farm because there is another one waiting for that to happen. Fight and strive and look and be confident that in the end the right thing will materialize.

A few "religious" people happen into this frame of mind and draw wrong conclusions. A Methodist minister may heal people or acquire all he wants, and he claims it to be because he believed in Christ his savior and thinks that a Hindu who prays to Shiva will never be able to do what he does. But they do, and even more often, (because there are more of them.) Those are universal opportunities, or you may say they are the only worthwhile things although our fathers and mothers and schools and churches and universities have generally no idea about it and never taught us. Yogis expresses it thus:

47

"Present education is dangerous. A Raja Yoga education for everybody is the thing." A Sufi may express himself in other ways. Both see that the general trend at this time and stage in civilization is blind, ignorant, "dangerous."

The whole secret about the duality in prayer is this: The Kingdom of God is within you. The only purpose of the Christ principle is realizing that You are Christ!! You yourself, your soul, heart, mind, body. That is all. No duality. The only Being is God the Creator - you and I.

Shamcher

April 17, 1975

Dear Carol,

May 7th I start on a trip, first stop in Houston, Texas, and from then on I don't know, so this is just to tell you that from the 7th of May I will be away from home for a while, maybe 5 days, maybe 50, maybe 500, who knows? It is a search for who knows, first a strange professional or business meet in Houston, and then ...

A triangle, with top up, red, flaming, lusciously red, only the upper top, not the whole triangle, sensing it, contemplating it, not sitting down, but while you work, cook for example, or wash dishes, and if you wish to expand it into one of your beautiful mandalas and then back again to the top of that red triangle - would you please tell me what this awakens in you, what thoughts, what feelings? Then, when you answer that, we may find out whether you should continue doing this or something else.

Carol, you are incomparable teacher, friend, and lover.

Shamcher

April 26, 1975

Dear Carol,

Your reaction to the triangle-pyramid was superb so far, and will go on superbly. I do not know yet what will happen after Houston but I shall telephone you whether I can come to Vancouver B.C., probably telephone you on Saturday May 10 or Sunday, so please send me your telephone number before I leave or phone it.

A friend wrote and asked me about retention of breath (hold it in so long,) what Inayat Khan has said about it. I replied that to my knowledge he had never advocated it. In addition, all good yogis know that only under constant guidance should that be done, by one who really knows all medical traps, and that, anyway one could reach God without it but might jeopardise reaching God because of it. So he said that, Oh, there were lots of papers showing that Inayat Khan favored it. So I wrote to him some letters about which the enclosed are the two last ones. I may have been a bit too emphatic I am afraid.

I do so appreciate your letters. I am closing now, for good reasons, and love you more and more.

LOVE

Bryn - Shamcher

P.S.I am pleased that you realize the implications of your new Love relation. It seems very important to me that you stick with the program, the rules you have made and which you told me. Very important. For everything.

April 22, 1975

Dear R__,

I have had the privilege of spading the ground for Sufi groups in fifty cities around the world, unnoticed by the busy-bees, and even taking part in the expansion of Murshid Sam Lewis' group in San Francisco from a Rihayat-Ruhayat to a blending of all Sufi groups in the face of resistance from so many worthy sources including, at one point, resistance from Sam himself; and here, Sitara (now ailing) and I have fought overwhelming odds - leaders who wandered into black magic, leaders who stopped short when I went on a mission for the United Nations, and finally we have two stable groups here, or three, M___'s, A___'s, who follows her line and is visited almost daily by Inayat Khan or versions of himself she can accept and enjoy, versions however who often tell her bluntly what she ought to hear. All of us have a version we can accept and, although I have been blessed by many, many of these versions, I humbly admit, that even I may have only a version. And now I greatly appreciate your coming here, for, in the first place, I may leave this area after my trip, and even if I don't, I look forward to your coming and our occasional co-operation. Only beware that you do not destroy, in building up.

The breathing we talked about - no, in no collective interviews I know of did Inayat Khan ever advocate retention of breath. His secretaries, who took down his words, were from all walks of life, theosophists, yogins, etc. who had a hard time reporting, and when he came to breath, they thought:

"Oh, yes, we know that," and wrote what they knew, not always what was said. The same applies to all papers, ryasats, etc Perhaps I should not have told you this, but now I did.

Love and admiration,

Shamcher

Report on reports and retention of breath
Fourth Installment.

April 24, 1975

Dear R__,

I know you have been waiting excitedly for this follow-up: Susanna Kjoesterud, Sufi leader in Norway, once said to Inayat Khan "But you said so, I read it in the papers, the report." Inayat looked at her with that utter compassion, "My dear Shaika, when you hear something directly from my own mouth, you know I said it." To some of us Inayat did not need to say that. We knew.

Some people meeting a man they don't like, put their noses in the sky and say: "We'll look him up." So they look in reports by Government agencies and Credit Bureaus and wallow in the muck and lies. It is not that bad with the Sufi papers and reports, though sometimes almost. Every single human is a source of endless nonsense. All reports, rules, laws, "established facts" are so much trash.

Yet one's duty is studying carefully whatever reports one wishes to study, with utter attention, yet again (and here comes the difference) with utter humility, knowing some or most of it may be worthless trash. If one strives for exactness along with this humility one may find a new vehicle. Most of the people who attended Inayat's lectures don't know as much as those who entered this other vehicle, though of course even if you did attend Inayat's lectures you still can enter that other vehicle. It is called Intuition, Divine Intuition. And I am telling you this because in your future there is definitely this possibility, if you grab it, the possibility of entering the gate of divine intuition. It will be a shock, but welcome in the end. Many things you now believe you'll have to discard. Your respect for all Sufi and other leaders, and top hats throughout history will change color and sense. So many mistakes were made throughout history, yet it does not matter, they were steps to achievement by others.

You may be able to follow all proceedings as they happened, and no longer depend on the little hieroglyphs we call letters and jumble together into sentences. You may see ditchdiggers having the larger vision than the Yogacharia, or, as happened when Shankaracharia looked over his crowd of upper class pupils: "Where is Singh?" Singh was the kitchen help. He wasn't really good enough but he was the best he could find to represent his teachings when he was leaving. For another world (which is still available to those who have entered the vehicle of intuition.)

Love,

Shamcher (the smallest among you)

May 6, 1975

Dear Carol,

From the enclosure you see that Hidayat is going to send you tapes of his music. This makes me seventh heaven happy. You received my letter that Saturday in Vancouver is out? Have to go to other meetings. Some other time.

Sufis are average people. Putting on the Sufi label does not make them (us) angels, does not even change us immediately. Just a longing, a hope that we add to life to make it richer.

A person watching the holy rollers, would he say: "Look at the Christians, that's how they are. Imbeciles." Do people say the same about Sufis just because some of their followers, or their teacher, are flailing around in ignorance? Nevertheless, I often asked Inayat Khan: "Why not drop the name Sufi, which is connected with so many historical blunders?" "Well," he said, "If one day we think so, let's do. Meanwhile, if we don't put a name on ourselves others will put a name on us, and it may be worse." Really, so many beautiful Sufis have lived and shown examples throughout history, Jesus, for example, that the Sufi name shouldn't frighten a keen observer.

No, the papers aren't all fakes, in fact very few are. I just wanted to make him a little less sure about the papers as compared with living matter. To his answer calling for a "scientific search" there is of course the answer: "What is science and who are the scientists?" Among the only qualified ones, such as Inayat Khan, these are not included in the scientific community, nor would want to be. Science knows nothing. A few scientists do know. The books are the same as the papers. I thought you had books.

Shaika means lady Shaik, a sort of organizer, corresponding to grade

10 in the Sufi Order. She may also be a teacher. The more specific teaching line is a Khalif, same degree, or Khalifa when a lady. Inayat Khan had four Murshidas, the only Murshid rank he ever gave at that time, to four ladies, no man. But I had to laugh over some of them. Titles may not be what they appear to be. They are in the Sufi tradition, that's all that can be said about them.

Yes, when I initiated you I was so told. By a voice. This whole letter may seem hurried. I am preparing for a strange journey.

I love you.

Shamcher

May 10, 1975

Dear my dear Shamcher,

Though I (inside somewhere) expected that we could not meet - still your phone call came as a shock to me. Yet I was pleased you had called today. I worked very long and hard and was resting when you called - Oh, Shamcher! It's not the time yet for me to not see you anymore. Something in our conversation gave me a very sad feeling and more than ever I feel a need to see you, to be with you at least once more. When you said I should be in contact with others about the papers whether you live or die that hit me in a place that caused a great sadness. For I know that you are older and that I will "live" much longer than you, that a greater part of my life will be spent after you are gone - but not yet, oh please. So, strangely, what I felt from your phone call wasn't disappointment at not meeting you, but another deeper feeling (one I felt with you a few times before) of the briefness of our contact, of the precious treasure of our relationship and of the tiny shining jewel which is like a melting snowflake in the sun. Evanescence and passing and changing. I don't tell you this asking for reassurance - or do I?

Also, when I said that I love you, you seemed to suggest that your feeling was perhaps stronger. This may be true, for your depth is far deeper and your height is much higher, so of course your sweet feelings are much finer and more true. Yet in whatever is my limited capacity oh how I do love you and care for you - please never think otherwise. However foolish I am, yet still I am true ... how could I not be when you are my very being.

I'm looking forward to the music from Hidayat - I am so very pleased that he is sending us a tape. Also I will write for the first three papers (although I am shy and don't know how to ask.)

Enough writing for now. Thank you for phoning me even if it was with sad news. Please take care. I suppose you won't get this letter until you return. Oh Shamcher - I can't express what I'm feeling - but you must have felt it as I was writing this and you can pick it up from the paper if that feeling wasn't consciously felt by you then. Now - as you read this keep this thought - our relationship is so very precious. I feel you as a melting snowflake and wish I could turn this snowflake into a permanent diamond.

Love,
Carol

I thought I was finished writing but the feelings keep pouring through to word them and put them into thought

What is it that I'm feeling? It's the constant change of this life. How do I feel it? As sadness and a pulling pain-like feeling. How can I get past this? By accepting it all as it comes and loving the moments.

Oh now why was there such a tearing in me at the phone call? Why did it seem so short - far too short? And I feel you're inaccessible (physically) for such a long time - I never even asked when you'd be back. Perhaps you could phone me when you are away. Perhaps I should get out of this dreamworld of what I want and just let it all go by. Who knows what I want or who I am or why I'm writing or who I'm writing to?

This is the time to let it go, to break the dam and let all the waters flow. Why hold back anything at all - let it all pour through with no impediment. Let it all flow out like a torrent of rain from the clouds - dispelling the clouds in the process and leaving all clear and calm and without motion.

I love this world but I have to let it go. I love this world but I can't let it rule me. I love this world but it's not my real life. God help me in this strange happy sorrow.

Carol

May 12, 1975

Dear Shamcher,

For some time now each day has opened some miracle to me. I find myself deeply intertwined with people, especially those who open - the contact goes very deep - but I don't know these waters at all and I ask you - when this deep contact occurs, is it right for me to act as I do? I find myself probing with my eyes - as if they are going into someone as deep as that person will allow, until a wall is hit, and it's on that level that we relate. I wonder, is this fair, or

53

right? How does the other person take this? Is he/she aware of this probing? These thoughts usually come after the time of contact. So with some persons there is an open contact, eye to eye and deep, yet a straightforward awareness of each other. In others I feel the wall, sometimes right on the surface, before any diving in at all. I don't break through any walls, but stop and relate there - do you understand what I'm explaining? It seems like a sense, but I can't say where I sense this "wall" or how or anything. But there is that exploring.

My good friend told me of an experience she had last week which seemed the same as what I experienced in San Anselmo. She had terrible pains and tears and contacted a tiny pained and screaming being way deep inside. I knew exactly what she meant and went through, though for her it was with dark screams whereas with me it was with deep tears in waves turning into laughter, then tears again. How can this little pained being be freed? It's like a baby that must be delivered.

That talk with her made me think that this exploration isn't all light and joy. Until the darkness is dispelled there are very dark times to go through - but strength of the light increases also. So I was thinking of that but not at all prepared for the "dream" which occurred. I was aware that the entire world was a dream and a trick, but the trickster of the world kept trying to get me back into it. He came to me in many forms - nice and teasing and cruel and all sorts and sometimes I was tricked but regained myself and was confused and scared but steadily kept to the light, concentrating on God - but as his attacks were increasing - scrambling my mind and paining my body, I lost all except the Lord's Prayer which was all I could grasp. So I repeated that over and over again and he was still around me but I was floating up above myself in a protective cloud of light. Then I woke up and it was intense with energy in the room - patterns in front of my eyes, cats yowling outside. I knew that if I went back to sleep, I'd go back there, so I continued to pray and as it eased I thought of you and asked for help and asked Inayat Khan for help and then fell soothed to sleep.

The next day I was totally exhausted.

My immediate thoughts are that I am more resolved to keep apart from the world in all that I do. I see it all as a trick. It was a heavy battle and it's not over; the same as that little being who must be delivered - there's more yet to come. So I ask you, dear Shamcher, what can I do to deal with these times? I seem to sense beforehand that some big one is coming through, but that's no help in the actual experience. I knew after that dream that the person I was fighting was the actual devil. Also, though it seems outside, all this takes place within me and wherever I am is projected in the world as my reality.

What happens next?

Love,

Carol

May 14, 1975

Oh Carol when Saturday evening came, the time I could have been with you my heart stood still and I was dreaming, and not altogether peacefully either, for a fire was raging that almost drove me mad.

Carol you must have been with me for thousands and thousands of years, becoming ever more dear, more close, more one with little me than even myself.

Bryn

May 15, 1975

Dear dear Shamcher,

What a fine phone call! I was in heaven for quite a while afterwards. And so perfect of you to call in the few minutes I was at home, at a time when I was experiencing such exhaustion and lostness - you heal me and give me such incredible strength and loving power - I cannot express the wonder. When you phone for reassurance you give so very much. Oh, I know it doesn't come from you, but when you move over, then wonders flow through.

I wonder, how can it be that you can love me as deeply as you do when I'm so limited and so faulty with so much to let go of and unlearn? When I think of some of the selfish things I've said or written to you I feel your great heart even more - for you know these things yet you love what is within. In the warmth of your great love I open and flower and shine to you - shining with a shining unknown to me, yet you bring out the best in me by your love.

Who are we? Why are we as we are? What is the reason for this union? If I were a knife to pierce your heart, I would pierce my own in that process and we would both disappear in one blow. If I were a star to burn you away, I would burn up also in that very instant. If you were a fire to burn me away, we would be a star for an instant as we were consumed in the blaze. If you were such a sword to pierce my heart then your own being would perish also. The single blow and there no more. If this pen were a laser and this paper your heart, you would feel each letter as it is tattooed forever, the light would shine through your heart to awaken your being and would shine this love through all.

These words amaze me, coming from the depth of this love. Once the inside is touched by the ray of your being, then out flow these words. I have no questions for you this time, no answers, just this flow of feelings translated to words - and in this realm where we are together travelling hand in hand, we are truly at home - ecstatically dissolved into each other - all atoms of body and mindstuff intermingled, all inner self radiant and united.

Oh if we were side by side now and I could look into your eyes and truly flow into you, filling you completely with this love.
Carol

May 17, 1975

Dear Shamcher,

During the week is no good for us to visit one another so this means we won't see each other for some time. Yet I love you so dearly and feel you so closely within me that I can wait. Although I can feel disappointed, I won't. I'll just look ahead to when we can meet in the future. Besides, this is the best time that there is.

Have you left me alone at this time to go through this great gate waiting all alone?

Oh Shamcher, you were wonderful on the phone - I was crying by the end of the call. The beauty of your great soul filled me with peace. I wish I could describe you to you, then you would know what it's like to be me and have the precious moments of knowing you. What we share is a marvelous loving - all the air between us is charged with it.

I wish I could flower out to you all that I feel for you, get in this letter it can't even be approached through the words. I so dearly love you. I could tend you like a tender plant. I could care for you in 1000 ways.

Please write soon, I've missed your letters, it's been a long time.
Lots of love,
Carol

June 1, 1975

Dear Shamcher,

O hello you fine fine one. I feel like writing everything I feel and have ever felt to you today - an energy and a joy I wish to share.

The weekend was a deep one - all Thursday and Friday night I was in tears. In a rush of experience I painfully remembered (as if I were there again) all that surrounded my son's death. Then in a flood came all the little memories of our life together - everything so tender, so fragile, so momentary, so forever gone. Just as a wave of tears would end, another wave would begin. Just waves of tears. Such an incredible release of feeling. Then friends, "helpful," came to distract me from the experience.

On Saturday came more tearful waves, touched off by reading a book by Laura Huxley all about her life with Aldous. I was so touched by the depth and breadth of their lives, by the incredible human potential for experience and expression - all that day I was in tears at the greatness of human existence and the transience of experience and the many levels all simultaneously part of each being.

Today my love for you is deeper than ever. The exercises are increasingly more meaningful to me, and I feel a stronger than ever commitment to the Sufi way, I want very much to learn the Universal Worship. Oh, there is so much to learn and so much to unlearn.

As to our great mutual loving which extends forever without end - what can I say? It is always in my heart. Your tender being, your strength, all of you is here in me.

You are beautiful.

Love,

Carol

June 9, 1975

Dear Shamcher,

Here is a question, I hope I can form it so you'll understand what I'm getting at. When I'm with people, I seem to get as close to them as they will allow. I respect their walls, but I probe as close to the walls as possible. How very very rare it is to deeply communicate with an open person. Sometimes I'm closed up, wrapped in myself or my idea of the person I'm with - but more and more it's as close as possible. Now there are people who have come to me asking about Sufism, or wanting to do the exercises or just deeply

57

communicating. With these people, who I feel so very responsible for, is it my responsibility to break down some of their cracking walls or do I let that happen as a natural outcome of the exercises, the openings, the changes? It pains me to see them locked in various walled ways of being.

Now I am just accepting, it all, and loving it all, and hoping that whatever the wall is will slowly fall away. I can't do anything like slashing the wall directly as we talk, or can I? I don't ever feel right in shaking anyone's reality, in pulling out the rug from anyone's feet. Yet you could say that the one they are attached to is not the true self and therefore the hurt doesn't matter. I feel strongly that I must respect all of a person, the false ego aspect as well as the true. I address myself to that true one - always - through the false, ignoring the false or letting it be. Yet it hurts me to see what little control there is and how the other covers the glimpse of the true.

So I've come to understand what I'm asking you in this note - is there any subtle practice I can do for these people to help bring out their true selves? I can't say anything when a dark spell is upon them, but I could help them on another level. When they're open, there is no need for words or practices, we just clearly meet and it is beautiful. Are there specific practices for specific personalities that I should know to give to the persons, or will it all just occur spontaneously and perhaps I am impatient? If there were such specific practices, would it be right for me to give someone a practice which I myself had not done?

Oh, this is all speculation at this point, but I know I must prepare and learn at the same time as unlearning all this for myself. In one of the books it says Inayat Khan said that you should beware of becoming a teacher while you are still a pupil. But aren't we always just at the beginning of the learning? It hasn't ended for you, learning from everyone and everything. We're all just beginning. But your beginning is so deep - the place you begin from is so far - your little voice on the phone was so beautiful. I say "little voice" because I think so tenderly and also because you were so gentle and open and humble and little it made me love you all the more.

Please write me soon with an answer, or if not the answer, then your answer to my philosophical speculations. I just go on what I feel at the time. Love,
Carol

June 12, 1975

Dear Carol,

Shamcher wanted me to let you know that he will be able to write you next week as Tuesday he had to go to the hospital for surgery. He had an annoying stone in his bladder and it had to come out and there must have been something else they did too as he was in the operating room for three hours but he is in the hands of a specialist and seems to be getting much better perceptibly.

You will have another child and your little son's soul who passed on to the next world will come and live with you all again.

Our grown-up son, Bryn, finishes his journalism course in college by a four-month apprenticeship in Pt. Orchard on a small paper there. Pt. Orchard is close enough that he can commute. When young Bryn is home his father's eyes light up like blue jewels because he is so proud of him.

Give our best to Gary. Shamcher expects to come home from the hospital Monday and wants to go back on his diet which will prevent him having to undergo any more surgical operations.

It is very beautiful here now and everyone is waiting to put in their garden in the middle of the month when the ground gets warm enough.
Sincerely,
Evelyn

June 15, 1975

Dear dearest darling,

Do become well so you can be strong in body as you are in spirit. From here I can send you all love, all caring and all of me to wish you what little I can. I won't send you this right away, I'll wait until I hear from you. Why? Because I am afraid of you dying and of this letter lying cold and unopened. Yet the very sending of this letter might draw you back.

I can't say to you - stay for my sake - for never will there be enough yet it is always enough. For me I can't honestly say "stay," yet for us all it's such a gift, your work, your life here. I say stay for the rest of us. Yet your death too will be a sad gift as your being is freed at last. (Though you have been free and so wonderfully working here for a long time now.) You were so kind on the phone, now I know why you were so particularly gentle. And this particular gentleness, this fine loving, I send you now with my deepest gratitude for your being. Yet now I feel that you must become well and remain working on earth for at least another 5 years. This is a crucial time and we are almost over the hill to the new times ahead. (What am I writing?) For us all you must remain here. Yet if it's time for you to go, you will live forever in my heart. And how many other hearts have you seeded? Within myself there you are! More love than can be here expressed comes to you now in this letter. The beauty we share, oh yes, it's shared with everyone, yet between us it is a very powerful yet immensely gentle experience. You taught me how to love and continue to open my heart wider than I believed possible.

Love,

Carol

June 16, 1975

Dear Carol,

Coming home and seeing my mail box for the first time since ten days; your two lovely letters soothed and lifted my soul and somewhat cut-up body and may be the reason why I am so much better. The much betterment started yesterday which may be when you received Evelyn's letter and sent me some of your smoothly healing sentiments. I will write, but now this has to go to the mail. Just to say: you are unique, a universal fire, but soft, such a blessing, wherever it falls.

Shamcher

June 17, 1975

Dear Carol,

Your close friends and your approach? First, of course you are not a "teacher" nor am I nor was I ever nor will I ever be. Whether you will be, I do not know. Inayat Khan was and acted a teacher and what he said was that don't act a teacher while you are really a beginner. I am at the beginning and anywhere else all the time. But in any meeting between two or more there is a constant interchange during which one is "teacher" (never thinking so) and a second later pupil and vice versa. And then you ask: should you shatter their superficiality or let it disappear gradually through practices? And then I think of the ones you mustn't touch and others you must shatter, immediately and effectively. You know when and where just as much as or better than I. There is a young man, very vain, whom I shattered and thought he would never come back. He came rushing back, again and again, and now says I am the only one he can trust.

You could do the following: When they talk uninteresting petties about themselves, don't answer. Just look intently at their heart. To them this lowered look will surprise and often offend and they may burst out, "But you aren't listening." Then you look up into their eyes and say, "No, I wasn't listening at all. Instead, I was looking at something so beautiful, so absorbing, I heard or saw nothing else." "What was that?" "Your own deep, beautiful heart, that part of you where you are one with me, with all living things..." You say nothing about the superficiality.

As for practice, you can give anyone an englishified zikar. Tell them to realize for 5 minutes every morning at a certain time, that in their heart is a great being who knows and sees all, but if they don't want to do it regularly, at given times, then tell them not to try at all, for obviously they don't seriously want to. I am a little tired and empty after my ordeal so I cannot write much more just now. Only tell you that your descriptions of your own feelings and experiences are beautiful, sensitive and marvelous, showing living progress.

As to myself, I am not available to anyone except Evelyn until July. First. If as you say you like to come to Silverdale after that, write or phone Evelyn.

Love,

Shamcher, Bryn

June 20, 1975

Dearest dear Shamcher,

How good it was to receive your note, so short but it contained so much feeling and warmth. I was encouraged to hear that you are feeling better and I pour my love to you continuously in wondrous streams to encircle you and warm you and heal you. This happens whether I'm conscious of it or not, for I encircle you within and without, shining!

Hidayat's music came today and I am very grateful for the depth he shares - how will I ever be able to thank him? He sent two pieces - *Invocation* and *La Monotonia*. Both very deep. How can I tell you what they did to me? They did to me what you do to me. And I couldn't help soaring and vibrating - I was light, shimmering light. I may never quite return to earth. His music is beautiful! Surely this is the time for it to be heard, recorded and shared with many people. It is so beautiful and moving, not on the surface, but far deeper/higher.

And you, what now? How long will you be recovering? Did you

know that this operation was coming? Each night before I go to sleep I sweep round and round you - why circles? Sometimes I come inside your body and shine out. Who am I then? Precious person I love you dearly, with such tenderness.

With great caring and a big kiss!

Carol

June 22, 1975

Dear Carol,

I know that you understand my reference to teachers in my last letter.

In the old Sufi traditions certain people were called teachers and Inayat Khan followed that pattern. To me there are no teachers, except God and nature, and Inayat Khan often said exactly that. My feeling, which I have no right to publicize, is that at the end of his life he no longer believed in the separation of teachers from pupils or in hierarchies. His second son, Hidayat, to whom I am very close, tells me that his father expressed that definitely before he went off to India, though Pir Vilayat cannot remember it. Faithfully, to his father's traditions, Pir Vilayat has built an organization on that pattern and it is for me to support him. But it is also my duty to make known my own deep feeling about this which I have done more successfully with you, I think, than with any other.

Other people who are close to me and close to this concept which I wish to be expanded as time goes on are... (a list of names and addresses follows.) Sometime in a hundred years you might interest yourself in some of these persons and their tasks.

A person who just hears about something does not claim to teach, but is from that moment often a more efficient real teacher than an old hand. Therefore, hierarchies or acting as teacher has no place in truth though may be applied for some practical reason, at least according to some.

I hope never for me.

Love,

Shamcher

P.S. Please write!

June 25, 1975

Dear Shamcher,

I'm writing you in tears for the depth of the wonder of this love which circulates through us all. After writing thank you to Hidayat (and if he will consent, some people at the radio station will play his music) I folded the letter and placed it in its envelope. Suddenly I was seized by deep tears and cried and cried to him (or whom?) wetting the bottom of the envelope and weeping so hard the inexpressible waves. This beautiful feeling pours through us all so marvelously - and it has nothing to do with the person at all, the person is its channel and the less there is of you the more there is of this wonderful flowing spirit.

Last night some people came to visit and I felt this spirit flow strongly between R___ and myself, yet he was unaware. I want to wake him up to himself. And how sad when there is no sharing of this spirit, yet how I love everyone so deeply and forever. Whatever is needed from me I will gladly give and more, yet I cannot be totally wide open with everyone for they wouldn't understand. Or can I be totally open with everyone? What do I do?

I love you so deeply and forever, my gratitude and respect for you grows each moment as I feel your being, remember your words, think of you. My heart is yours and I breathe your fine being with each breath, and this moment and forever we are only one. And this one is not just us two, but is everyone's essential nature. This spirit of flowing love has no beginning and no end and is all-pervading and marvelous.

More than anything I want to be totally gone that this all-flow can take me forever. I wish to close my eyes and fall backwards into the sea of love, dissolve totally.

Love,
Carol

July 3, 1975

Dear Carol,

Your beautiful portrayal of your reaction to Hidayat's music made my day. I quoted you in my letter to him. I am writing this at the office. The first two days of my return I finished all the work that had heaped up on my desk, which they told me "no one else could do." Now I feel silly and overpaid. Three weeks back work finished in one and a half days. And a whole nation and a world to be rescued, saved, corrected and they know it not. They have the "officials" who bumble from day to day without any view of what could and should be done. And I have to sit here.

You said in a letter you could not open up to everybody? I always try to do just that, open up, to everybody. But many resist. Then I try harder. What one says is another thing. A great art: to say just the thing that will open them up in return. One has to be careful, thoughtful, and above all, in-feeling. Sometimes one cannot say anything. Inayat Khan especially often said nothing. Sometimes I felt he didn't say enough, try enough. But who am I? I don't exist as you know.

I know you will have gone from Edmonton now, on your great trek west, and get this insignificant mail when you return. You may have phoned me or not, visited me or not. You know, I never feel I can be of any use to anybody. You came prompted by a tremendous urge and made your own values. If you ask others to come, they will be very disappointed. Especially in view of you having built me up, far far beyond my worth or deserve. I do not even exist, remember? Actually, I am so convinced of everybody having their own great teacher in their insides, knowing so much better than any outsider what you should do, think, initiate, that an outsider, advisor or oracle is not called for. So why should anyone come here?

Besides, the gremlins of a hospital's operating room have still part hold of my body. I am depleted and fight a modest battle for survival. I see it in all my dreams, strange beings, small monsters, attacking and being gently torn out and away, a process demanding your energy and attention, to the detriment of anyone coming, hoping to take part in the tremendous stream I was once putting out constantly. I may even be on my way to California, any moment, without warning (to or from myself.) Carol, you are marvelous, quite great and strong already, ready to take on the world.
Thank you! You don't know what good, what great you have done me.
Shamcher

July 3, 1975

Dear Shamcher,

It was so good to hear from you again and to know that you are back at work and recovering. You know, you are such a dear friend - I just wish to share some time and space with you. And if you agree, we will come out next weekend or the weekend after. If you must go suddenly I'll find out because

I'll phone first. Also, if you don't feel it's right that we come, you should write me right away.

Next fall I'm going to work setting up a group to make change in the laws about midwifery so that women in Canada will be able to have safe home deliveries. Also to change the situation in hospitals. I've helped in this a bit last year, and really feel that this is an important issue and this is now the time for such a change. Perhaps babies born more humanely and less mechanically will be more secure and able to cope with the world as it will be in the future.

- this love has no end,
Carol

July 9, 1975

Dear Carol,

Thank you for the lovely fairy card, so I reply with a bird card, closest relatives. To think that you are much closer already. What privilege.

Really, I can see no reason why you should leave beautiful Canada, even for a day, to come down to commonplace no-exciting Silverdale, and our stable where we live, or exist. Besides, your great friends and life companions may have a fairly decent impression of our humble family here if you don't spoil it all by showing them the actual article.

I am in a strange limbo between two worlds, the one we "live" in here, and the one we live in hereafter. It is really very much the same, except, of course, that in the afterworld we are less exposed to the freaks and dangers of this world. But there are other freaks and dangers, much less organized, more variety, more "uncertainty." (Oh, how the good ministers would shake their heads and raise their forefingers to such a statement. Except those who know.)

Carol, you are wonderful and you are safe and encompassing large areas of all worlds. Thank you.

Love,
Shamcher

July 11, 1975

Dear Carol,

Your letter from Falkland was very interesting, especially that you are buying land and I can look forward to your being so much closer, only 260

65

miles from Silverdale. As I read the map, Falkland is about 20 miles north-west of Vernon, about 5 miles straight east of Westwold and I understand that it may be hot. Have you anywhere to swim very close? What are you going to grow or what animal are you having? Goats? Goat milk and cheese are much preferable to cow milk and cheese for most people and the goats can be kept roaming, which is so much better for them and their products, but you must have your vegetable gardens fenced in (don't fence in the goats. I don't like being fenced in either, I am to some extent now.)

My enormous strength is coming back so I can say that if you feel I should receive some of you, well, it may not hurt you-all too much, but we will see when the time comes what Evelyn says.

My unbridled curiosity: What do you pay for land there? If there are any houses, what do you pay for the whole shebang? How many acres or square kilometer or whatever? For we have thought sometimes of acquiring land too. But I would like to be near the rolling ocean. My weakness. One of many.

Love,

Shamcher, Bryn, X-15

July 20, 1975

Dear Shamcher,

What is there to say to you to express all that has been bubbling outside and inside since the visit? To tell you is hardly adequate. I feel so foolish to tell you all that I feel - for in this last visit I was younger than any other time, and surely more humbled.

Any error in regarding this as a "personal" love is very clear. And yet it is even more a personal love, but with such vastness beyond and within. These words simply cannot say it.

All the way home my mind was full of so many thoughts - when we were together I didn't seem to think much at all. It seems like I'm the same as when I first came to see you, only worse, with more blocks and such foolishness! I see so many blocks to expression within me and I am so tied up in my own ideas of "what's what" and so closed that it takes a sharp knife continually trying to pry me open! How I wish to shine spontaneously with the true light!

It's as if I were a child - all-there-is stands shining before me but I am clumsy and foolish. The feeling: even when I thought I wasn't, I was

66

identified with the wrong self, or external me I think I am, not the eternal one within. Isn't that the root of the trouble, the mixed-up thinking and feeling? Oh, I would do anything to erase the damage done by the selfishness! Constantly it's there and how often I forget, then turn around to see myself acting selfishly, without care or consideration and my heart breaks again.

I've been going along being submissive with people rather than responsive. I have been abdicating my responsibility (just realized that "responsibility" and "responsive" are of the same root) to our true self by often going along not making waves in a situation that is directionless or downhill. What a balance, then, between the strength and the controlling or taming of the ego part.

I think, oh, how can you stand me so selfish and terrible, then I remember: That one is not me so I let it all go and learn and carry on. You see through the clouds to the sunshine. I feel like such a baby beginner in this world, in these realms of being, yet there are sure feelings that I trust so deeply. One is that I am yours forever. Yet you always give me back to myself. Is it this that shows me how?

What do I mean to say? Is it that I am more dedicated to this way of Sufism than ever before? No, it is that I want to go through all of that; to travel in "Sufism" but to go through, clear through even those ideas and concepts. The goal is to be totally free, and I will follow this Sufi way as it has unfolded within and without me as the only way I can do it - including all religious ways, shining the light.

I see this whole letter as unreal in a sense, or after the fact, a sorting and sifting. All I express here has already happened, yet in the writing of this letter, more waves are sent out.

Something else: this "passing of the baraka." While you were in the bathroom, A___ took my hands, thumbs up, etc. and held them for a while. Did the same with Gary. Now it seems to me that this passing of baraka occurs spontaneously all the time, it's just a matter of perceiving it. But am I wrong here? Is there more power in a controlled transmission (through the body and vibrations as tools to this?) Does such a practice (the formal doing of it) open a person to receive/perceive the spontaneous forever flow?

How beautiful when we were in the car and I couldn't do anything but share all with you as I turned and your eyes were more beautiful, your beaming as we shared such beauty. How kind and clear you are, and so very very gentle with me. With a swift blow my heart opened and during the tears then, and only then, I was open enough to begin to begin.

Thank you so much for everything! I truly appreciate the strong fragile gift of your beautiful self.

Love,

Carol

P.S. The prayers with motions are most beautiful and deepen daily. Just the perfect expression of what I wish to say. A gentle dance hardly moving the air but making beautiful waves!

July 28, 1975

Dear Carol,

Thank you for the fine letter, showing your exquisite ability to transfer your thought and feelings and soul to paper. You are not quite right in your lamenting about your selfishness and guilt and all that, and at a later age when your physical power has diminished there is the danger that you may turn around on all the people you have admired and accuse them of all kind of omission and commission crimes. But you seem into meditation and may avoid that stupid danger of accusing your surroundings instead of yourself, and really, you shouldn't accuse yourself either.

But what is meditation? Not just thinking, in fact the opposite. There are two ways of meditation: voiding the mind of all appetites, for food, for sex, for fame, for riches, for achievements. Or concentrating on one point - a star, a guru. The modern way of concentrating upon a guru may create all kinds of difficulties. It is still a form of appetite. But the guru's physical form is not the real guru, but rather his spirit, or rather than that again, your own spirit, inspired by the guru, whether he deserves it or not.

This also answers your question about the thumb up transmission of physical force. For people living on that level it becomes important. Also, it may prevent them from advancing further. But it is not necessary that it so prevents a being, if that being can free himself from it later. In a sense it is like drugs. A person may be on a stage where he would never have had a lift except first by drugs, but drugs also prevent him from going on. Except if one day he can free himself entirely from the delusion of drugs. As to such transfers of physical force - to an enlightened being it is no help at all, just a cause for an indulgent smile. To a physically drowned person it may be temporarily good. Again, it may later prevent him from going on.

And you see, a Sufi does not necessarily live in stables like me. The very advanced Sufis may live in palaces, like Rumi. Or in deserts without even a tent like Shams-tabriz. Or a Himalayan cave, or on a Himalayan crag.

Gary was a new and gratifying acquaintance, a real true Sufi whatever he calls himself or does not call himself. A good companion for you.

Love,
Shamcher

August 3, 1975

Dear Shamcher,

Hello! I was hoping to hear from you today - golden letter - but the mail held only flyers and advertisements. So much has happened and I need your advice. Perhaps just writing to you will help, already I have been drawing on you.

Last night I "dreamt" that I was going away, as everything was gone, and I flew out of myself entirely. I thought strongly of you and then of Inayat Khan and then - I was gone (I can't say where or how) until I returned, first in a dream of the place seen from above, within the consciousness of everyone here and from myself sleeping and from the trees; all at once hovering; then awake in the body. That's at night.

In the day so much has happened. Friends have arrived and we have been working hard. To describe what I feel/see of you now is foolish, for I perceive as much of you as I am able to perceive. Only that. All I say of "you" I also say of "me," for in "me" are the perceptions of those aspects of "you" - yet we are essentially one shining sun - just one!

Oh, Shamcher, - I could cry and cry for all the feelings that roar through. I felt the same at Sitara's house, such tender feelings - all the experiences we beings go through and all the tenderness, loving, the hurts and little fears. We're all just children, opening the hard shells that pains have left behind, so that we can become more. These feelings are greater than anything in the world that we think is real, they resound further and deeper. All I am is this. To feel this is to cry and cry, but not in a hard cold pain, in a gentle loving tenderness.

I was going to write "I'll close now" to end this letter, but I won't "close" now, I'd rather stay open!

69

Lots of love,
Carol

August 5, 1975

Dear Carol,

You are beginning to travel in your subtler spheres or bodies, which is a great blessing and source of knowledge when done discriminately. And for this to be a blessing and not a nightmare it is absolutely necessary to conduct your physical life according to discriminate principles.

Every generation hops up and down and thinks: We are free and superior to our stupid parents and ancestors who were uptight.

Ha.

I have seen this again and again for how many times? But it is simply this: At all ages and times there are immature young souls who seek pleasure, and older more advanced and comprehensive souls who seek more pleasure, the pleasure of the Universe, of all, for a grand exciting future goal, against which all smaller pleasures vanish. Sometimes these smaller pleasures have to be cut out quickly and absolutely and it is no fault if some one is hurt because he can't have short pleasure. In fact, you help him (beside yourself and world) by hurting him, and deeply.

Anyone who comes barging in on you while you develop the finer senses because he really loves himself and his passion more than he loves you and your whole vast personality (which he cannot yet know) has to be cut down with all energy at your command. There are great teachers who push their pupils down hills when they rush up too grossly.

There is a fine, subtle, elegant touch to all things, sex (which does not even exist as a separate entity) love, feelings, and bless you, find the subtle game. Oh Carol, you have such a tremendous future, now, here, in this life, please keep to it...

Love,
Shamcher

August 11, 1975

Dear Carol,

Thank you for beautiful letter. I shall quote your words about your *Monotonia* crying in my letter to Hidayat. I enclose Hidayat's letter to me from which you see that you are free to use his music on the radio in Canada and without charge. If a remuneration of any kind could be arranged, very

70

good. But it is more important to have it played, even if nothing can be paid now. You see he is also sending you some more records.

I also enclose two talks combined into one by Inayat Khan, and since this is my only copy I would appreciate it back some time. Also, since the mail to Falkland seems to be a bit erratic - a note from you saying you received all this.

I am going on a trip, will be back end of month. I have so much more to say but you know already.

Love to both,

Shamcher - Bryn - that other fellow-all

P.S. Thank you for a fine photo of you in our garden.

August 11, 1975

Dear revered divine music-soul Hidayat Inayat,

Thank you for your lovely letter. I am conveying your precious information for Carol Sill to her in a letter. She just wrote me from her vacation in Western Canada:

"I would like to write again to Hidayat, but his address is back at home. I wish to tell him that when I was driving I was in a sort of dreaming state and the *Monotonia* began to play in my mind and I was humming it. It was beautiful. Then I began to think of my son's death, thinking of how I felt at that time, of what he went through, and I found myself crying the *Monotonia* instead of humming it, and that was even more beautiful, for the tones just carry the waves of tears and feelings so perfectly... it was a good release. I suppose there is no need to tell him of this, but at the time I wanted to thank him."

I feel these words of Carol are such a proof of the power of your music.

What you say about the Sufi work touches me very deeply. I feel that our common feeling and understanding should be expressed ... not as a substitute for whatever else is done in the name of the Message, but as an addition, an addition which we owe to the latest feeling of your beloved father. For in the beginning, he, too, had the titles and the hierarchy, as had many Sufi organizations throughout history, and maybe people need that, at a certain stage and that it will attract masses of people and that it is destined to be...in addition to our precious view. I feel I would never want to fail in my devotion to and appreciation of Pir Vilayat and all his followers and whatever other views and systems there are. But I also feel you and I have a sacred duty to clarify and gather the people who share our view. Many are very responsive to these ideas which I never hide but neither do I press them upon anybody. And I think Pir Vilayat has great sympathy for them but also sees them as not covering all aspects or all groups of people carrying the Message. In short, I feel it can be done while retaining deep respect for all factions, all people, particularly those who live and fight for the Message under whatever form.

Beloved Hidayat, may I in all humility name you a precious soul mate.
Shamcher

August 13, 1975

Dear dearest Shamcher,

Last night we went out for dinner and I began to talk and talk and talk, what was I saying? I'm not really sure. Talk and cry and talk and cry some more. Gary was confused by my behavior (so was I) but once the talking and crying was over - or the wave that caused it was over - or is it better to say that this talking/crying was the body/mind response to the wave that was bursting through?) it all came, though what "it" is can't be worded. After that I was talking more only not confused - certain that who I am and what I am must be expressed. This is difficult for me to write now, as I am the "me" of this moment.

I feel on the edge of a big change. I have nothing left to hold back - "take me" is part of this feeling. I want it all to just pour through without any of me in the way at all. Enough fiddling around self-consciously with my toes dabbling on the edge of the water - dive in! Each time I dive in I think I've done it, but then find somehow that I must walk further to the water and dive in again. It's like the tide goes out as I jump and yet this time it's a deeper dive and this is deeper than ever.

Gary couldn't understand just what I was expressing so he went to bed, and then the wave of it all broke - whoomph - onto the other side. I felt that I AM in a way never before. The prayers are so redundant when I am saying them to myself! I am the one I am praying to so what I must do is manifest and be. No holding back. It's like I broke through myself and there I was. How can words express this? I wanted to tell you this, for reasons I can't say, but to you I wanted to sing some of this because Here I Am.

72

Then after that instantaneous recognition I went to the living room and picked up a book and these words jumped out off the page: "Concentration requires voluntary attention." I thought this over and over and it is so very true. Now this sings through me and in everything I do I see that concentration requires voluntary attention. My involuntary attention to all around distracts but the voluntary attention placed in each circumstance or moment gives great peace.

Last night seems like a promise of what is to be. I am at the beginning of a great wave of change like no other I have ever experienced. I feel within me such a power as I daren't express. Yet to you I can openly say that this *me* is limitless and infinite and to say I am alpha and omega and the spirit of guidance is it - especially the part about the heart constantly reaching upwards and speaking words put into lips as the light fills the crescent moon. Today I felt a glimpse again and little me is astonished and terrified and amazed yet I have always known that the time to shine has come and so I will always be manifest. We are so beautifully one in this work yet how can any words tell anything except a hint.

I just re-read the part "I feel within me such a power as I daren't express" yet the power I feel is the expression of this power and strength which is so infinitely clear. I am the sun.

Time is different than it was before. Sometimes I wish I could be with you to say these things. In the light of your great beauty I feel myself flowering to resemble the sun which you are. I am amazed in this transformation of the flesh into spirit. (And spirit is really first so it's just a return to essence.)
Love,
Carol

All at once I am nothing and everything and all in between is this marvelous universe. When I write it's so limiting and limited but I must write - when I speak to you it's also to me and what I say sometimes pours through and I am amazed. Each instant is a total new creation of the entire universe, yet each instant flicks through so fast. Such a marvel of continuous creation/ destruction! The beauty of being - to connect/be this source, and the beauty never ends, it flows forever. At the same time such peace - but why do I write this to you? My incessant need to express, create, and word it all. I want to express so much, to share and to spark the light in all around me.

To you I send this as a word picture of what/who I am at this time. To give myself in the feelings in the words. And the self I give you is the self you showed me when we first met as you drew from me (or who I thought I was) the light that was nestled curled away within. Once the opening is made and the light pours through, then forever shining it increases the opening until the sun is blinding in its brightness.

A part of me says "Help, am I insane?" But the beauty and strength is too great to be tricked or stopped in the flow. Last night the voice of "Help am I insane?" was totally gone and the light shone clear and unfiltered.

This letter is already too long, I ended it once but longwindedness got the better of me - one word should sufficiently say all that I really want to tell you - LOVE.

Carol

Also, if you are ever travelling anywhere at all, for any reason, I would love to accompany you. I'd love to do this and really would expect nothing except to be with you for a time.

August 26, 1975

Dear wonderful exciting thrilling Carol,

In your sumptuous letter in which your magic word power holds me spellbound, I nearly flipped when you wrote about travelling together. Travelling with you? What festive thought. I sigh, I weep, I laugh, I explode, expand to high heaven merely by the thought. But how could we do that, when they all expect us to arrive single, just for them? Since all our hosts have lovely emotional trends and look at each one of us as their bridegroom or bride respectively, and this is all because of their loving divine nature, how could we disappoint them and come wound together almost like a couple?

Carol, my feelings for you cannot be measured any longer and I am almost afraid, but what a delicious fear.

Say, did you get my letter with copies of letter from Hidayat and of my letter to Hidayat? You did not tell me yet.

Total love,

Shamcher

P.S. About that other gentleman: it seems as if you accept his manner with equanimity. It seems to me that you avoid your duty to impress a less evolved soul with the consideration and restraint required for growth. You are his teacher, not his lover; one mistake is forgiven, two not so easily. Are you going to waste a lifetime?

August 29, 1975

Dear Shamcher,

Your most recent letter has so deeply affected me in a way I couldn't describe - except to say that your strength and vigor and power knocked me over into 1000 backwards somersaults in the air and back again laughing and smiling to you! Your visit to Cleveland must have been a very fine one! Of course you are absolutely right about the travelling - but keep me in mind the next time you go somewhere - it may or may not be as you say.

Yes, your letter knocked me out. And Hidayat's music is deeper this time - he sent the quartet of which the *Monotonia* is part - how can I tell him how subtly the music teaches? It opened depths unknown and anything I say is like a raindrop to the ocean.

Today I met a friend for lunch. We talked, and soon we were just looking at each other very clearly, sharing the beauty of being. He reacted very much to this and became weak in his body and felt a lot of physical changes. I was just sitting there, loving the beauty of his shining self soul - of me/you/all/us--shimmering. To me this was not an overwhelming thing - I could feel when it was too much, when we should stop, etc.

Why is it that my experience is like this - I'm not interested in anything at the time, my body feels normal, we share that beauty and it's marvelous but it feels so natural to me and not overwhelming. I can focus in on any other mode immediately - turn to talk with a passerby or drive the car. Is it that a part of me is not totally letting go? Or is it that my body doesn't happen to react in such an involuntary total change? I had to sort of hold him up as we walked home. To me it didn't seem like anything that extraordinary was taking place, yet to him it was as if I were sending fire through the glance.

So I'm asking you: is it that I'm holding back and not letting the power all pass through or is my body somehow used to this or made for this and doesn't feel it foreign or shocking? Or am I in another part just keeping a control on the situation to keep it all in line?

How foolish these little questions could seem to you, these little after-the-fact wonderings. But if I analyze what has happened then it's stored for next time and hopefully I won't make any of the old mistakes, just new ones.

Now when I pray it has turned into a song of sorts, without music, but a song all the same. Your letter was so full that I had to answer right away.

Such fine feeling fills me and pours to you in an unending stream.
Carol

August 30, 1975

Dearest Shamcher,

I'm writing to ask if my girlfriend and I could come and visit soon.

It's as if the cycle has come round again, and I think so dearly of you. The last letters show part of the changes, but please know that these letters are only captured moments frozen in expression for this time - I move on, changing, growing, but the letter stays forever, as the moments stay forever. There is so much I must discuss with you - to write it would take pages and pages. I need very much to learn from your experience in these realms - you who love so deeply, so perfectly and so tenderly strong! My admiration for you grows daily and my little understanding of what-it-all-is constantly revises itself to new forms.

Oh Shamcher, how can I say what these past days have been? There has been no time - the day has not been morning/afternoon/evening - it has just been experience upon experience. How many days in one day? And I don't sleep. The body rests and rejuvenates but my life-experience continues on other planes and day and night are one. Dream life enhances, completes and continues waking life and daily life affects dream life. The energy shooting through is most powerful - the love pouring and circulating through us all is so very strong and beautiful. I have so much to learn and so far to go and this moment itself contains so much!

So much I wish to talk with you of: about Sufism and about love, about the changes we all go through, and about you. You can help me so much by your gentle being and kind big love.

This deep unfolding seems to be unending. The waves are so beautiful. How can I learn except by experiencing it all step by step? And as I catch on to something, then at the same time some other part is let go. Always I write this sort of thought and feeling to you - now I am plunged in deeper and far over my head, though my heart keeps me afloat. If I use just my head, I'll drown for sure! what happens now?
Love,
Carol

September 2, 1975

Dear Carol,

Yes, of course your glance can bring up or down the mightiest giant, why does that surprize you? Whose is it, really? And it will go on, and become more mighty, if used as intended by those all-powerful forces that are now yours - as long as you act in accordance with them, which we call wisely.

Your letter was beautiful beautiful, swelled my throat.

And now you and your friend are coming? Please phone about it, whether you come or not, so we don't have to stay home and wait if you don't come and won't be away if you do. Shall we go to Raymond, or to the ocean and swim? I would like to write more, but I can't and mail is off.
Love,
Shamcher

June 29, 1975

Dear T___,

Your letter is encouraging in that you are wondering about the boggle of questions in your mind and all the answers you thought you had. So you haven't got them any longer? Congratulations. For there are no real answers until all you have "learned" drops from your mind like useless toys. That's when intuition begins. And you don't "understand" it all. If you understand it, it isn't intuition. But all your life your schools, your school mathematics, history, geography, physics, psychics, maybe your parents too, taught you to respect your logic, your "learning", so how can you suddenly laugh at it? Most people have a terrible time, never get there. But they may try again.

The one you describe has no "gift" that you don't have yourself, but you have said fine, I agree, I am with you, and now you are back to the same old structures and logic and questions and answers, or are you?

In a huge library in California (where the Sufis had many retreats) a Chinese proverb adorns the wall: "True wisdom" (intuition) "cannot be found in any book." Nor in any brain for that matter, if we define brain as most western scientists do. Intuition is another world altogether. But it is your world. It is in you. It is you. It is not a gift. It is yourself. And who knows himself? If you think you do, you may be sure you don't. Don't even try. Just live, and tell yourself. You will be what you tell yourself. Nothing else. You, as well as your brother, know this. You certainly don't need to ask me. Carol Sill knows it too. A 26 year old girl. Not everybody knows it, not yet, but eventually all will.

When you have questions you may ask them, but the answer comes sooner if you don't ask, just laugh at your naivete in asking. The answer is inside yourself. But people make lots of money on the fake supposition that they can tell you, come to them, come to the Himalaya primadonnas, come to the Master, come to the chaplain - oh, some of them even believe this themselves.

Asked dervish Abduh of theologian Abdurrashid of Adana,"What's your view of 'inner knowledge'?" "I have no patience with it." "And what else?" "It makes me sick!" "And what else?" "The idea is revolting." "How interesting that a logical and trained mind like yours, when asked for a view on a matter, can only describe three personal moods."

Hopalong Cassidy, come home.

When a dervish says "I do not exist," that is not affectation.

Shamcher

September 10, 1975

Dear Carol,

Please add this to the copy of letter to R___ which I sent you and receive a great relief: Forget about the tape recorder. I found one here at the station, took it with me into the secret hideout, played all three tapes so that the rhythms seeped out and made over every blessed soul sitting at his desk or sweating at his work bench. So there.

But I cannot take this recorder out and play the tapes for you. And I discovered that the reel tape recorder is 100 times as big or heavy as the cassette recorder which I have, so it would have been a giant imposition on you to have you bring all that big a thing.

And what do you know? I still love you. Or is it you? Or me? Is it just that God loves himself, herself, itself??? We'll settle that one when we meet.

Love,

Shamcher

September 10, 1975

Dear R___,

And of course I had to forget the most essential in my last letter to you: That of course Pir Vilayat does communicate, constantly and effectively, though not all catches on in their daily consciousness but in their sub and superconscious they do catch on; for every morning and every meeting, and often after, he communicates directly. And from his present standpoint that seems often sufficient even though his communicators may not always realize this.

To wit, and love,
Shamcher

September 16, 1975

Dear Shamcher,
oh shamcher, my heart -

My thanks can hardly express my gratitude for the splendid visit. I feel that the main body of this letter is unsaid - the essential love which is us and ALL. The love that we are is all that is real - I touch you through the air just by being - this phrase reminds me of a poem:

GRACE

0 unending fountain of love and of light
radiating within us deep forces of joy
our mouths sing the praise
our eyes shine the light
our hearts send the love
dear unending fountain of love's own deep light
o beautiful blossom of grace neverending
all you are sings your praise
just by being

Love,
Carol
P.S. Am I your daughter, lover, mother, sister, friend, pupil, teacher or yourself? Surely I am you. This language limits so much as it expresses.

September 19, 1975

Dear Carol,
After your lovely and loving visit, your and M__'s, all you can think of in your sweet conscious-striken feeling is what wrong you may have done with the tapes, but this was all my fault you know, or maybe fate, who knows.

For I became aware that I probably should not have even mentioned to other Sufis in the U.S. that I had three tapes, and I phoned from San Francisco or anywhere else, for reasons that were not under my control, but my "forgetfulness" may have been engineered from somewhere for the benefit of - who knows?

When your check for 31 came tumbling out of your letter I thought first of sending it back, but the Sufis say "give what you have and accept what is given you'! so there you see how dangerous it is to send me checks: I accept them. With many thanks. But actually, while I was paying that bill I thought: How much should I now pay Carol and M__ for part of their other trip expenses? But since my checking account was very strained and I had just had all kinds of expenses with Bryn and Daphne my mind conveniently told me: Pay nothing more for now.

Have you learned how to be on top of your strength at all times even if a vampire-like being pulls all your sap out of you? For this is not the fault of that "vampire-like" being, if you lose your strength. It is your own fault. There are some who accuse innocent little beings of drawing out all their strength. I say. "Do I draw out your strength?" "Oh, no, Shamcher, on the contrary, you charge me. That's why I sought you in the first place." "Well then," said I, "Now I shall draw out of you your strength so you can accuse me." And I never have been forgiven. I didn't mean to draw it out permanently, I just emptied him for a second, trying to teach how to charge from within. Some do not want to learn.

The device is simple enough: Just tell yourself, and feel the charge entering and filling you. This protects you from communicative diseases too.

You are precious, Carol. But the separation early Sunday had to be. And my greetings and thanks to M__. And to Gary who let you come.
Love
Shamcher

Carol: Your second letter just arrived. The dearest ever. Please write. Don't stop because "you know it all". Even if I did, I love to hear it. By the way, your friend? yes, that is her nature, to drop out and in. Nothing to worry about. But natures can be changed and often are.

September 24, 1975

Dear Shamcher,

So pleasing to hear from you again after so long. Right now I'm in a spell of writing writing writing all sorts of things, pages just pouring out without a stop. The day is just so beautiful, each little detail so precious, every moment a jewel of such wonder - like breathing, isn't it? In and out, the waves.

Your letter was timely and perfect. It seems like such a cryptic impossible communication, these few words. If I could fly to you this moment what then would I express to you except a kiss and wide opening, entirely wordless and perfectly beautiful. You are forever in my heart and whatever I can do for you, I will do without halt or question.

Learning of how to keep up strength is of course very valuable and something I've been trying to find in my own way. Certainly the other person or persons are never at fault, for we are all as we are. Who is then "at fault" except perhaps me - I can work to change myself. Blaming others for my own clouding is one trait which requires work. More and more, the world I'm in is showing itself to be my own creation.

We move soon, and I'm beginning to pack boxes, yet all the while there is this explosion of ideas in my head. clarification of concepts, ideas of shimmering beauty, all coming to the forefront of consciousness, eclipsing all else in their strength.

Please write to me soon and often, for your letters are so beautifully good - its not what they say really, or whatever is intended in meaning, but the strong feelings and you-ness which I drink entirely in each letter. Please tell me some of your feelings and thoughts, and whatever else flows through your mind and heart. You know, I would recognize you any time and in any form and in any situation - for you shine through your being like a bright light through a lampshade.
Be well and remain happy,
Carol

September 26, 1975

Dearest Shamcher,

To continue our continuous letter - our entire correspondence is a dance in the air. About your writing: it is fantastic. If you have the time to begin a new work, even just a few articles, it would be so clear and beautiful, for you could begin where you left off with your last book. Writing assuming all ideas are accepted and just going deeper and deeper into the essence of your understanding (or do I say translation?) of reality - all of itness.

You know, the time spent with you was more beautiful than ever before. You were so filled and flowing with love and joy and peace. In my caring for you, it is all of everyone I care for - your particular expression of us/it/him who resonates within. There is no way I can say now how I felt, but there's always the knowledge that this is completely understood. How unnecessary these words are - just decoration.

What I learn from you is how to act in this world, how to deal rightly - in this the learning never ends - we are embodied and in the bargain the tension between spirit and matter continues unending. The beauty of living in the spirit is to marvel at the wonders of matter dancing to the unheard tune. Why should I write these things to you when you really planted the seeds of all these thoughts? The seeds already existed dormant within, you showed your sunshine and they awakened. Nurtured by the sun which is all, how marvelously deep this life is. And how much farther we all have to go. Please remember how tenderly nestled in my heart is a little Shamcher. And this could be called by any name you like.

May my love for you sustain you now on earth and in the hereafter - take whatever you need from me, for the fountain you have awakened will never run dry. Though really your needs are all met from within, so just joyously run under the sparkling showers. The fountains of our souls meet and the waters mingle to flow to the ocean of being. I am yours and you are my darling.

Love,
Carol

September 29, 1975

Dearest Shamcher,

I'm sitting in the autumn sun. How do I feel about Sufism? I would let it go in an instant if Reality shines. Sufism and all around it mean nothing yet also everything. The practices are beautiful, yet not "it" and all around everything is beating around the bush. I see where I could organize a great Sufi group here in Edmonton but is that best? That's not at all what I want to do: I only want to be free.

Going to the bookstore yesterday all I saw were reams and reams of books beating around the bush. The cyclone around the unseen centre. What stuck out most was 8 copies of *What the Buddha Taught*. Why did I laugh and cry at the same moment seeing 8 copies of this probably fine book? Will any buyer find what the Buddha taught after reading this book, so many hundreds of years after the Truth of Buddha's experience (whose experience?) And I'm so very sad and so very happy. Nothing is important to me right now, yet I seem more involved in things and events than ever before. The blocks within me are revealing themselves daily, and that work never seems to end. Yet within is the great feeling that all is one and the unfolding of the wonder is such a beauty.

Everything seems to be falling away! It surprizes me that even Sufism goes (though from this point of view it is not surprizing but natural.) Here I am on the ride as the universe turns itself inside out. More and more I expect less and less of other people and more of myself. So much to let go - this heavy mask (it doesn't need to be heavy though.) Who am I? Nothing really. If I can just be harmoniously or should I say totally, with whoever I am with, just be them and see from their eyes, then surely all would be at peace.

What are the changes? one part of me asks. Knowing their names stops me from flowing from one to the other. "Oh, that - that is bla-bla-bla." How does it help, filling up with more and more concepts?

This isn't any different from any other letter you have received from me - aren't we really just saying and stating and restating and asking and answering the same thing over and over again in everchanging forms? So this is the first letter I've written to you, or the 3rd, or the 27th, all the same. The writing continues to bubble through, weaving pattern after pattern, version after version of the same story. Yet it deepens. It is love.

Oh Shamcher, the vastness of all, the beauty of all is incredible, yet somehow I don't care, not in the old way of caring. I feel when I am with people that I am both them and myself.

Last night I dreamt you showed me all sorts of practices, which we did and the states were marvelous. I was surprized in the dream that we did this. I awoke as satisfied as if we had seen each other, and so we did. Enough words now - accept my love, caring and eternal gratitude - also a kiss in the air.

Love,
Carol

October 6, 1975

Dear Carol,

So perfect are your letters, so full of all the treasures that make up life and your personality that I have nothing to say now, nothing to answer, all just blessed silence, the music of silence. You are all set to leisurely build a beautiful organization while laughing at yourself and being blessed by those you built it for. Now I only have to tell you about some dumb mistakes I made. In one letter I said Pir Vilayat was following Gnana Yoga, the wisdom line. He was. He is beyond that now to a blessed combination of all lines - Gnana, Bhakti and Karma - wisdom, devotion and action. Even in ancient times the *Ishopanishad* said: Don't waste your time worrying whether you are in one of these lines. That stops you and you can't go on. You are in all and you must realize you are in all.

I enclose some other dumb letters.

Did I ever tell you about the meditation group? I hope I did, so I don't need to write about it. It would be unpleasant writing. If somebody is already in it, don't say anything, except if they wonder and ask. If they are not yet in but wonder about entering, warn them. There are other avenues of yogi. Good avenues. Many young aspirants in it are good and fine, for they have not yet reached up into the realm of muck. Never insult them by warning. Only when they begin to wonder themselves.

Oh my. I have already written a few words, and not all of them pleasant either. What you write is always pleasant. And deep.

I am revising my unpublished books and will send you a copy.
Carol you are a wonder in my life, and in any life you come in touch with.
Love,
Shamcher
P.S. Someone wrote me about titles, etc. "I don't understand this. What's the problem? If Inayat had meant no titles, no hierarchies, he would have told Pir Vilayat who is always in touch with his father, so where is the problem?"
So the enclosed.

October 2 1975

Dear B___,

Through ancient times the authorities were so cruel the Sufis and others had to teach pupils to obey and no nonsense. The Sufis had mock hierarchies to be acceptable to the worldly powers of mock hierarchies. I have more experience with hierarchies in business, government, and religious organizations. One of my little duties is to gently help the new trend along when there is a question.

Pir Vilayat is right in using titles, since many need it and demand it. His brother is right in stressing the coming trend. Otherwise the Sufis might eventually work against the will of God. I am with both Pir Vilayat and Hidayat. I see both. Pir Vilayat also sees both. There is no problem but a challenge. One of many. Pir Vilayat and I can never be in disagreement. We both live in another world than talk. But occasionally we come down to talk and then there may be an appearance (to the ignorant) of a difference - because we have talked to different people at different times, which, who, need different advice.

Yes, Inayat Khan is not only in constant touch with Pir Vilayat but with all of us, as God himself is, and we catch what we can and no more. And his being in touch means that he gives to each what each should need just now, his special message to the world. For "the Message" is not a pat set of words. It is a thousand messages, delivered by each one of us, in our own way.

You indicate that I am stirring things up. Not for the stirring, but for truth, and sometimes truth is stirring but that part is not my concern. Don't worry about the stirrings. If someone bawls you out because you have followed your conscience, enjoy his confusion. You cannot help smile. Your clearer vision may eventually reach him.

love,

Shamcher

P.S. Talk this over with anyone if you wish, but in that case, show him the letter so he sees what it is all about, and don't try to condense it in a few words of your own which would not give the picture.

September 3, 1975

Dear C__,

From Chicago base I took a brief trip to Cleveland and had so hoped to see you, to hear about Chamonix and all. I was there before it was a Sufi camp and retreat, was carried aloft by a gondola my engineering eye told would crash, and so it did - later. But I left a thought up there and, lo, marvelous Pir Vilayat built a camp. I wondered ever since if I would ever get a chance to go there and experience it. When I phoned you I was impressed that you had an answering service, a sign of efficient work which I should learn from.

I am particularly glad that you are such a good friend of Pir Vilayat, who so brilliantly is organizing the Sufi effort, doing things that nobody else I know could do. The Sufi activities are now functioning better than governments, despite the fact that the governments can offer paid work as an incentive. All criticism of the Sufi activities are just by people who focus on lesser issues. Some seem to think that because a person becomes a Sufi he (she) will suddenly be an obedient, slavish puppet. The wonder is that we do operate with all our individual glories and adornments and idiosyncracies.

I have known Pir Vilayat since he was ten years old and I was 29 and even then he was in many respects my teacher, though he always looked to me as one. People who want to tear us apart tell me that we don't agree, but there has never been even a sign of disagreement between us. People tell me that we disagree on titles and hierarchies. Not at all. We both know that any organization built here on earth must have degrees, titles, a full-blown hierarchy. Sufis always knew and acted accordingly. We also both know that in Heaven it looks differently. As a great Sufi of the past said, "The first shall be last and last shall be first," or that which is so serious and so necessary in an earthly activity is a jubilant joke in Heaven and to God.

I look forward to meeting you in person, beyond your answering service, at some other time - maybe in Chamonix!
Love and admiration,
Shamcher

October 2, 1975

Dearest Shamcher,

So much went through me catalyzed by your letter - I'll try to tell you some of this now that there is a moment's rest from the moving of all the household. Oh dear darlingest one! The Sufi work is spontaneously going on no matter what I do, and really, one (or may I say all?) of my greatest joys on earth is to see this marvelous spirit of beauty and peace spread and awaken all the sleeping souls to come and take possession of their rightful kingdom here now on earth. Perhaps the setups I have seen have turned me away from organization, though it was a joy to see so many people together. And do what I will, people are gathering here, too, slowly - but I wouldn't want to rush it.

Since I have moved here, the bookstores now sell Inayat Khan's books and I have heard of lots of interest in Sufism. The people I have been connected with in deep contacts spontaneously are Sufis already, and immediately respond to the books and the teachings without me having to do anything at all. In this, is there a need of an actual formal initiation, or is the deep contact (heart to heart recognition) enough? Should I wait until asked, or suggest, or what? Some people don't really know that there is anything to do with "Sufism" at all, we just connect and it is beautiful, beyond words.

So some of the work is already spontaneously occurring. But what else can I do? I would hold Gatha classes with the papers, as many do, but really I have never even attended such classes so I don't know what goes on. Could you please tell me or suggest what can be done in this regard? What I am wondering is this: are these for "initiates" or for the general interested public? (What is the difference? Some persons so deep and splendid are not, to themselves, Sufis, others are "Sufis" to themselves, yet have so very far to go.)

What is done? I know the prayers always accompany the reading.

What is a suggested way of study - meditation on it, discussion, etc? What is the order of the prayers?

I don't want to begin going about this in a clumsy way not fitting to the work, so please tell me anything that you feel may help. Also, if more people are drawn to the energy circle, like rays or ripples going out which increases the people who are ready to feel it, and they too increase the energy - what do I do with them except share what I can, talk, and give them the books. Yet am I ready for this?

If someone should need a specific practice, I know only of those you have given me. Yet I've read in *Toward the One* many others - are these of help? I need to know how and why they are used and in what circumstances and for what temperament before any such suggestion.

And similarly, the Universal Worship Service, which could be easily performed. But again I am unprepared. I find it beautiful to worship and the freedom of being within the framework allows the same dance to unfold new each time. It could be so joyful, and perhaps through it more people who are interested could find out a little about what the Sufis do. Please let me know what I must learn to prepare myself for this.

It seems that what is needed here is to make contact and find out what Sufism is about. Also a need for people who are involved (however peripherally) to express this involvement. Also - what is the benefit of such a group? Support, increased awareness, joyful sharing and deep communion.

But still, Shamcher, I feel unprepared and unaware. Yet I will try and work as you said, then stand back and see what has happened. I so need your help and suggestions about how to begin this new phase - I see it as a heightened phase of the already growing process and I would never drop out of it - it is simply not possible. Part of the process of growth within me is its expression, the sharing of it and the spreading.

Your letter really brought all the feelings together and in a sense inaugurated this new area of even more consciously working to help us all to wake up.

So much more to say ......

Love,

Carol

October 10, 1975

Dear dear Carol,

Yes, you have the perfect concept! "Organize" just as it is convenient - and acceptable. No services in your home if Gary does not want it, but services in any home where they want it, or in a more or less public place if many want it, but not all in any one home. No initiations if nobody wants it or asks for it. If somebody asks, tell them, "Yes, there is," and they can have it if they want it. If they say: "Puff, what kind of organisation or religion is that, nothing definite, nothing sacred?" You reply, "If you wish to live in superstition and support of mock authority you will find a place for yourself. You may even have all that in the Sufis if you want to. But frankly, you may feel better in some more rigid place. Good luck!" But if they sincerely want to be Sufi-initiated, do, if you feel like it.

You are quite right, you have Sufi already and maybe nothing needs to be added or should be added, although always things are added as time flies. I would be most happy if your Sufi is a little different, less rigid, less formal than most groups are now, realizing that all initiations and titles are play, for the benefit of the playful. There is nothing wrong in being playful, it may even be helpful. But it is better to recognize it for what it is.

You could have more music at your comings together than Sufis usually have now. Singing, singing the blessings of various religions, for example. You could walk, run, exercise and picnic in the name of Sufi. You

88

could act socially and connect it with Sufi. You could talk or organize in all the churches and in the agnostic or witch covens if you like. Embrace all of humanity, all viewpoints. They are only viewpoints, aren't they? When you see, you laugh at all that. You are already creating a beautiful Sufi effort, different from everything and anything that has ever been, in my and yours, no I mean yours and my image and plaything.

In classes you are supposed to read Gathas, silence first and after, and then depart. It seems hard. Some prefer to have questions and discussions after. But only after a proper silence (no longer than anyone can accept) between the class and the discussion. Inayat Khan himself preferred no discussion at or even after classes. Take some other time for discussions. Prayers? You use them as much as you like with the classes or no prayers at all if some prefer that. (Some people are against learned prayers. Even some of Inayat's pupils, for example Paul Reps, who became a Zen Buddhist.)

If some people don't know there is anything to do with Sufism and don't want to "do," respect that, ask them to do nothing. Those who want to "do," encourage them to, help them do. That is Sufism.

Love,

Shamcher

Be completely confident. You are a more advanced Sufi than almost anyone you have met. You are free to act, as you see it. Don't worry about rules and usages. Except when you meet people who want you to worry about it. Then pretend to worry but don't actually worry even then.

October 11, 1975

Dear Shamcher,

Your letter came today, filled with so much and bowled me right over! Why? It was entirely beyond the words, though they too are dear to me. And as if the letter weren't enough, you enclosed the copies of other letters which opened further my understanding of all that is happening around you right now. My goodness! I feel on the fringe of it all, for I only know these people by reference or by letter; how can I comment? Yet I feel somehow directly involved in this and in every way I wish to help - to bring harmony to the people who are/were upset, and to come to a clearer understanding myself. My Sufi activity is so limited and I am a baby in all this, but in any way I could help, please let me know.

How remarkable it all is, these relationships in the air! And you are so skilled and so very right in all you say - to each one as it is needed. And in your total agreement with both so-called factions, which are (seen from above) both the ends of the same pole seen from different points of view.

Certainly this is the viewpoint needed if the Sufi effort is to grow and not stagnate. I, of course, don't even know what these various degrees and such are, not their names, nor their worth or value. In this I can be of so little help to you, though my heart is forever yours. I send what support I can.

Have you got my letter with questions about what do I do now? Please if you could answer some of the questions. I await your reply before beginning. It seems I ask a lot in this letter - you know you needn't reply to everything, as I'm sure you won't have to - but the questions that strike, please answer. I feel in another stage and I suppose I'm kind of unsure about procedures and all. I know I can make up my own, yet I feel it is important to keep as much as possible to Inayat Khan's original intention.

And here also is another thought - we are growing and evolving continually, developing the entire world slowly - how can we stay stuck even at what Inayat Khan channelled - we must evolve and progress, as surely he did through his lifetime period and does now. This is a time of great flux and change and we must be ready for all that is to come. If the Sufi organization simply cannot change, then there will be others on earth who will do the Sufis' work, with another name or no name, and "Sufism" as such will bog down in ritual and dogma. This is, you see, a time for rapid action as especially the American young people often become far too attached to ideas, symbols and names as if they were the reality, rather than that which is beyond. We must, in all ways, open this entirely and hopefully the organization is now ready for such a change. What will happen now is that the group which exists in its fine shape as an organization is now ready for the next step. If it takes this step, the growth and flowering will be remarkable, but if there is fear of change, then others on earth will take the responsibility. The essential Sufism will always continue, with or without the "Sufis."

I am most amazed and very interested in what was just written. It flowed out effortlessly and I read it as it was going by. How beautiful! The part underlined is very important and it seems to be what Inayat Khan had always intended.

Lots of love,

Carol

October 17, 1975

Dear Carol,

How infinitely much is contained in those two simple words: Dear Carol. Your monumental letter of Thursday evening came and it was obviously written before I had joyfully accepted all your actions. And explained how Inayat Khan did the Gatha Classes and how you can do them and all that. The only thing I did not mention was exercises - practices. Not all people need or should have exercises. Again, when they ask, give them. All the exercises you have now could be given to anyone (one of them, I mean, not many at a time) except the red pyramid, which is for you especially and is not even Sufi-originated. Exercises often have a good effect but often it does not seem to have the effect indicated and people become weary. The zikar develops love and in an aggressive and immature youth may express itself too physically. Give with care. Use the English instead of the Arab words (this is not my body, it is the temple of God. Mind. Heart. Soul.) The morning breathing exercises are good for everybody, are shared by Sufis, yogis and many others.

Your page five? It is excellent. Yes, but a bit too definite for my taste, thinking of the reluctance of many to change as required. It is more like this: Titles will continue perhaps forever, for those who crave them, but Sufi as such will also include groups with no titles, (and I dearly hope yours will be such a one) so that the future will include Sufis but certainly also many others, or Sufis not using that name. By the way, letters apart, Pir Vilayat and I do quite well communicating directly (just as you and I) though sometimes there are kinks in the wires. Yet, truly, your page five expresses Inayat Khan's voice through you and we shall some day do something with it.

Write and tell all, dear incomparable Carol, and greetings to Gary and friends.

Shamcher

P.S. More of my time goes to tell the Washington officials about energy and economy. Did you know that I happened to bring the Ocean Thermal Difference energy system alone to the U.S. in 1947 and now it is blooming into our one and only?

October 18, 1975

Dear (dear dear dear) Carol,

With your mail strike I understand I should not send you that book copy yet? It would not merely be delayed, it might get lost in the shuffle?

You know, there must be no feeling of pressure, not even of a desire, that is just it. No action - let action come, without doing. Your page five of that letter is an example of what will happen at least in some areas if our views are not at least admitted as part of the Sufi picture. It will show that this is not either Hidayat's or my invention but a mighty trend ... and perhaps the best trend. As you so truly said: Inayat Khan developed, as all of us do, and he frankly admitted this. Others tend to make him a born God, unchangeable like the universal laws (which laws? They are changeable, too.)

A dear friend San Francisco way tells me his prayers aren't heard, his life is in shambles, I am the only one who makes sense to him and yet even I am different. One feels like rushing right to him. Letters can do so little. I may send you a copy of part of his letter for when you meet similar souls.

LOVE (what word can show?)

Shamcher

October 25, 1975

My dearest Shamcher,

I have no words now, and truly can only say to you in this letter that I love you and respect you more than anyone could believe possible. All the feelings and unfeelings within and without are new and so very very alive. It is all alive and very aware. Here I sit writing, yet just a vehicle for what is pouring through. On Saturday night your presence was so beautifully clear - yes, yes, yes, is all I can say and I can speak no more about it.

Who are we then? In truth we are all and we are nothing, we are the creator and we are only beginning to be - so much but words filter it too much. Enough said. I am you.

The present - this is the present - to now integrate and live this knowledge while the imposter tries to get back to where she thought was home. In other words, perhaps clearer: work on the ego never ends. And how really easy it is: we don't exist at all - what you have said to me and I have believed is now a living experience. My God - I am bewildered and blasted apart yet only You exist - living the zikar.

Looking around me I see everyone around me, everything happening so beautifully - relationships, experiences, and it's as if I'm not even there. At first this was jolting and frightening, then letting go it was so clear.

Everyone speaks such wisdom. The current of life is us all! I want so much to work yet there is nothing to be done. Even before I think it, all is happening around me. But I'm not here. And it's as if I am a mind and around me are all the arms and legs. Such a remarkable thing - I don't have to do anything at all, just observe and of course be - expressing when I do and at this point marvelling, marvelling loving in a way never known before and oh astonishment! The whole world is one marvelous being - world within world - never ends. Love is our being. Forever forever so it will be.

Love,

Carol

P.S. Please forgive the wildness of this letter, in all humility I only can serve - nothing more and all is service, all is worship. Forgive my present limited understanding - it will become clear in time; I so trust the guidance - I must only let go enough to listen.

December 4, 1975

Dear Shamcher,

I returned home to find that I hadn't left you behind at all, for there was a letter you had written before the mail strike waiting for me!

How beautiful it all is! Thank you for the good visit and your kindness putting up with my miserable cold (or is it really a cold? Seems to me it was triggered elsewhere.) So much correspondence to catch up on - yet I write first of all (always) to dearest you, with whatever greetings and love a letter can hold.

Please come here sometime to visit us. Oh - so many thoughts and feelings since the visit. They range from total grand plans - these thoughts radiate and radiate - to thinking (or not-thinking) what does it all matter? This instant is/contains all - moment by moment all precious jewels yet nothing at all. Simultaneous everythingness and nothingness, this "reality" as one facet of it all, as good a version as any. Each person with their own self-created world of experience and feelings. So flowing in all these experiences, which are really only one ocean of being, I returned home to the activities and concerns here.

And as for you, dear you, it was so fine to see you, I mean to really see you those brief moments when the walls melted away and there was such shining. Forgive me any foolishness or strange behavior. When I'm with you

93

I become sort of helpless and lose my whole heart to your strong being. You were so subtle this time - what wines were pouring through? It seemed to me as bewildering as the first time I visited you - beautiful, attracting, compelling, love-filled, yet totally unknown, like another land.

I felt this time such subtlety - aspects never known before (not known due to my own clumsy vibration in the way) - because of feeling this fineness, it wasn't breath-taking or exhilarating, this feeling is too fine for those kinds of effects. I wasn't swept off my feet because we began in the air and flew further. I didn't worry about catching my breath because I was no longer breathing.

I haven't had a chance yet to get to your manuscript, and I look forward to diving into your spirit expressed in this writing. Isn't it great to be getting into the rhythm of regular correspondence again? We meet forever in the air. And what is it anyways except the one being writing, reading, loving, laughing, crying, being - through what we think is "us".
Love,
Carol

I am forever grateful to you for your sweet being and divine presence and love.
Adding to this letter before it's mailed:

All day Saturday, Sunday and also today I have lost my voice entirely. I think I have laryinghitis - a marvelous opportunity to "drop out" of continuous action into observation of the waves and currents of human interaction. How beautiful to see the silent influences at work! What is learned is just a grateful appreciation of each moment, without rush or the push to do, be, or be heard. In this, I trust that the lessons learned will remain.

In the past days I've noticed beautifully some of the subtle effects of being with you. Once again the world I thought was the world has now disappeared in the broader, deeper, richer world.

"I love you" is all I can express at this time. Let my self now fly to you to encircle you in this deep love - and may it evaporate through the stars to fill every being with the joy of their own nature.
Love,
Carol

December 11, 1975

Dear Shamcher,

I have a voice again! How things have changed! How I have changed - not only are circumstances mirroring this change, but my reactions to the circumstances show that there is a profound difference in being. About so many things I just don't care, they don't touch me at all. What would have sent me into a flap a year ago rolls like water down a duck's back. And my language is changing too: I seem to be incorporating more beings (how to express this?) my personality doesn't include just "me" at all. Life is the same as always, yet my reactions are very different. It seems that the divine inspiration, when it pours through, is most gentle to me. I find myself speaking words unexpected and true, but to those around me there is no hint of "mediumship", it seems like me, it is me.

My rhythm seems entirely changed, and I feel more ordinary than ever before. People soar and fly all around me and I sit ordinary, appreciating all the beauties and wonders they display. Time is different again, and yet all is more "ordinary" and smooth than ever before. I've been writing letters - and here I'm fairly wild - very straight-forwardly, a surprizing straight-forward style.

And as I learn it all, all over again, I write to you in a state like no other. Truly we are one - these masks fall and melt in the bright sunlight to reveal One being actively functioning in love and beauty - All.

Love,
Carol

December 16, 1975

Dear dear dear dearest Carol,

Not only are your letters like a storm of the universes, recalling to me again your whole indescribable personality, but they reveal in some sense even more than your majestic physical presence, show me more depth, wideness, color, music. Couldn't you make a rule of making copies and then one day publish them simply under the title, *Letters*? They would be swallowed up by the billions. If you like you could use some answers to secure the continuity.

You asked me for that letter and so I have to send it though I have never done this sort of thing before (sending another's letter to another) so I suppose I have to ask you to send it back and show (his) to no one. He was looking for a lady who would be constantly his, without any special effort on his part. I had written him how impossible this wish was and why. That, in fact, we never even know what is in the next second, and that at least one must constantly assure the other part in order to hope for any kind of attachment lasting. I spent last weekend in his area, around San Francisco. He chauffeured me all around, invited me to live with his friends. The hostess had said, "No, I don't want to see another Sufi." Then he showed her my enclosed letter. Then she said, "Oh, I must see him." We collapsed in each other's arms. She wants me to come back immediately.

I also talked at a Universal Worship north of San Francisco. It was a most beautifully arranged Universal Worship, far out in the country, hundreds in attendance. After each lighting of the candle to represent a certain religion, there was mass dancing and chanting of the holy chants of that particular religion, the whole congregation moving and dancing ecstatically. I have never seen it before. As you so wisely say: First consult, then come to me, then finally do the San Francisco variety. I can tell you something about that. I also corrected one thing. The cherag stood squarely before the altar. I never remarked on that but in my talk I told about the symbology: The cherag stands at the side, not absorbing the congregation's devotions but standing aside so it can go direct to God, not through the "priest". He came up afterwards and thanked me, saying he had never understood why the cherag should stand at a side.

You are perfectly right that your friend should do no Sufi practices. She is under the guidance of other spirits, good, charming spirits which however, are somewhat jealous of her and do not want too much interference by us. There are many like that, and they, and their guides, should be respected and we should humbly listen to them and act accordingly. We have just had a similar thing here, with some Sufis from Jerusalem. I had to use all my diplomacy, all my humbleness to straighten it out. You, Carol, have no such jealous guides. Whatever you have are so invisible, so utterly self-effacing, we can never be harmed by anyone or any thing, we need not be afraid of assuming any role, accepting any practice.

Don't ever worry about the above-mentioned possibilities. You have enough intuition to feel it whenever you try to give anyone a practice. It is soon enough to correct, when you discover it. You discover it by that flick of the eyelid, that little painful doubt expressed.

Carol, you are beautiful, you are tremendous, all and the whole of you. I never knew I should meet such a one as you. Thank you, oh Carol thank you so.

LOVE,

Shamcher

October 18, 1975

Dear D____,

Your letter could have been written by me - during the thirties. Except that I had no one to write such letters to. And also, I did not pray useless prayers because I never prayed. Until I found out the prayer was not to an outside person or being, a "third person" but simply a gentle reminder to your own real self. I had heard that, but I did not really know it, what it meant, until in my seventies. Should you then wait until the seventies? Of course not. You are ahead of me. You may get there now, this minute, or two seconds ago. I may be weird, for I expect nothing of anybody, in fact, look calmly for the worst. If anybody shows any sense, constancy, even compassion, it bowls me over. I get so thankful I can hardly stand on my feet.

In Los Angeles as I roamed the Pacific Pallisades, dreaming and dead tired, no job, no income; a nice car with a beautiful woman stopped and asked the way to Santa Monica. Wondering desperately whether I might ask her to drive me there (where my humble room was, and where I could hardly get up the strength to walk) I decided that no, that would be unconstitutional. So, tired, patiently, I explained to her how to reach Santa Monica and let her go. Now, thirty years later, I realize that she probably stopped to have a little adventure, fun, and me, idiot, didn't understand at all. Such is life, full of opportunities you don't see.

Finally a friend took me to the dunes where I lived as a beachcomber happily on one dollar a week. That dollar was for milk. Clams came out of the Pacific, some of them were exchanged for vegetables. I felt I could never get back into the pulsating life of jobs. Before I knew it, I had, and I wonder if it hadn't been better to stay. This was at the little town of Oceano, 12 miles south of San Luis Obispo, on the ocean.

As to women, I not only see that their feelings are shifting and that you can never trust constancy, but I see this in myself too. I meet women that I think I cannot live without, and mostly I have to live completely without them, but in the rare case where you are admitted to her courtyard, and you know her better, you find that you, yourself have changed - to nothing or to a new mate.

And sometimes you feel that you have thousands, all at the same time, and it makes you dizzy. But by the right words you may keep them devoted, constant, and at a relatively safe distance. And you realize the tentative, experimental stage of the world. After a million years there may be - civilization. Today we have immature experimenting. And a lot of pretenders who live fictions. So what? Enjoy what you can, bear the rest. There is nothing, in today's science or religion, that has anything but a lick and a promise. There are great individuals - a whole 1/1000 percent of humanity - the rest: children, playmates. The Lord is in all of them of course, but he isn't yet mature in all of them.

That's why we have and need change and hope it will be in the right direction, and work for that.

Love,

Shamcher

December 17, 1975

Dearest ever in my heart Shamcher,

I've been reading your book *Fairy Tales are True* and it is like riding through your mind. I am enveloped in your diversity of being - so many facets gleaming at once on all levels (or is there just one?) Just one where it all shines. The feeling is that something must be done to share your books! All together, what a picture of existence they must show. And words can so barely hint at what must be expressed. What can we do? Wait and see. Work and hope. All will happen as it should.

A question - what can I do about being strong, or should I say right on, or sword-swift or true while I so readily and automatically become whoever I am with? What is the balance? I see that to mirror is not always the best, yet my natural tendency is to mirror and not separate myself from whoever I'm with. I ride with them and become them. But this reinforces the reality they are in and I wish to lead people out of certain negative spaces. How then, can I keep enough selfishness to master a negative situation, yet still remain open? Contact and deep communication seem not enough. But then, "I" can't do anything. Perhaps what I'm feeling is not so much the question of how does it happen, but rather the awareness that it is possible and in fact the beginnings of this arising. And arising out of the simple joy of contact and swimming in it all, into the air of knowing how to let the current be guided. Not doing it, but it happening through me. Does this make any sense to you?

I seem to have found the answer to my own question - when I write to you am I just writing to myself? Your answer to this question may be deeper, or from a side I can't yet see. Remember, know, feel that I love you.
Love,
Carol

December 20, 1975

Dear Carol,

Beloved. Looking over your fabulous letters (which I send enclosed for your coming book) I have more monumental joy than when looking at a land-seascape of unimaginable beauty, more thrill than in the hottest embrace, more taste than eating divine food or drinking delightful juices, more, more... I'm not a very orderly type. These are what I found. Gopi Krishna would say, "Well, this is what happens when two people's kundalini have risen through all the centers and reached the final top chakra." Orthodox psychiatrists would just say, "Oh, well, in love every kind of imagination dominates." And God himself laughs and weeps because two humans have found him in themselves.

How how how Carol, can I end this letter? How can I possibly find a word that expresses my feelings? Impossible of course, so, just,
Love,
Shamcher

December 22, 1975

My dearest Shamcher,

How beautiful to hear from you at last after so long. I'm swimming in the power of your letter - all the diffusion of love you cannot help but include. So much to say - the inner voice becomes more and more clear - though sometimes I'm too infatuated with what I'm doing to hear. I feel so confident in this guidance that, when I hear, I do whatever is asked of me. This comes not just from inside, or thoughts, but also from outside circumstances or someone will speak and it will ring in me.

When you said I should one day publish these letters, I felt it to be true. Yet there is no copy of this letter, and all that I've sent before. Sent to you my dearest over a year of mad writing and worded confusions mixed with inspirations. With your marvelous responses. A book - what a tender, and so very very open flower it would be - I wonder how shy, how attached I

99

am to it all - if you would do it, I would – or perhaps this amazing tale is for your eyes alone?

A few days ago came an astonishing flash - looking at us all and feeling we don't exist. Either we are being blindly mechanically driven by forces beyond us (for most people, normal reality) or we are so in love that we are gone! All appeared as a swirling of forces, currents through us all. I don't want to be blindly subject to all the many forces that influence all the time - I wish to choose just what I participate in. In this I trust totally the guidance and learn/unlearn as I go. Goodbye for now....

Love,

Carol

1976
INTUITION, NOT TECHNIQUES

What do you think I know? Nothing at all and that, exact-
ly, is my strength. There is one who knows so much about
yoga, talks in a stream for three hours and people swoon.
He starts out saying one cannot really talk about yoga.
He should have left it at that. He talks about the wheel of
reincarnation, lending stupid dogmas to his listeners. Is
this what you want to acquire? Your whole mature play
(and mine) is just that we don't know - don't know in the
sense that we have learned in school to "Know" - know
that 2 plus 2 makes 4. Does it? Of course not.

Shamcher

January 2, 1976

Dearest dear Shamcher,

How remarkable the whole of life is! What amazes me is the depth and breadth of experience - the height of highs and depth of lows and all the spectra in between all directions. And it is you who channelled the love which sparked and sparkles it all - and to you I am so very very forever grateful and more than this - connected so deeply that I don't consider us separate beings but truly one, acting and working as one, different in one way of looking but seen as I see us we are only one. Who are you? or me? Who is anyone? It's a clear channel once opened and the contact is direct.

A friend asked me if I knew any way he could get in touch with you, to go to see you and I knew at that moment that he could meet you through me. He said he had some questions he needs answered and in my paying attention to him some power or force changed his state of consciousness very startlingly - answering his questions in a way he never expected. I felt nothing during this awareness, but a wish to somehow help him, a probing to find his needs. So he suddenly changed and my attention went elsewhere. An interesting flow, so smooth and gentle. He never told "me" his questions because I am not really his idea of a "holy" person as I'm not old or famous or anything. I don't know if he feels they are answered or if they are still important to him.

Yet there is this feeling coming closer and closer of being totally gone - just flying through all minds and still acting the part of myself, enjoying it and letting go more and more of what I thought was "me". Each time more flows through and I only see this from the results, like the wind seen in the trees - so with the unseen force flowing through us all, visible through all of us, the circumstances and beings.

So dear Shamcher, to you I send all love, all dearness, all caring with whatever warmth you can receive in a letter like this - to tell you these feelings is simply not necessary, for we are one; in my dreams you are so often present - last night so strongly I was filled with your being. Every night is as each day - a marvelous opportunity to explore and learn and discover. What are we? Such a marvel, as we are both inside and outside one another and at the same time one. About Sufi studies - studies shouldn't be like learning but something deeper than what most of us call learning - something felt rather than only thought. Like catalyst crystals which transform the solution they are dropped into. Seed crystal thoughts.

102

But it is late at night now and I must go to sleep. Writing this now to you feels like the first few times I wrote to you. This seems brand new, this letter to you, and the feeling I send you now is as clear as the sunlight. Send me anything at all - a few words or books or all your letters - treasures of the beautiful expression of your soul. If you were a diamond and I were the sun I would enfold you like you were a child, inside the sun you would dwell.

Love,

Carol

January 8, 1976

Carol, you beloved, you did it again, drowned me in the universes, in which we were one and with it/them. The perfect experience.

Since your friend did not write me, he obviously had his questions answered, through your initial agency. If he still has them, or if they are back, he'll write. But no sense saying that to him if he does not ask again. For if you say it now, this may drop him back to where he was before that event. My address, of course, is no secret. But if it can happen the way you described in this letter, that is better, more complete, more perfect, more exact. And more fun.

Oh how I like your symbols. And no less do I like the real things they represent or symbolize. Oh how you spoil me, dear effervescent Carol. (I have my own sublime feel about the word effervescent. Now I looked it up in the dictionary. It says "Giving off gas bubbles, bubbling up, foaming." No no, that is not my feel about it. It continues "2: Lively and highspirited, vivacious." Well, that is getting there, but this is only a weak indication. There is much much more, all the universes zooming into life. Isn't it nice to have our own vocabulary? Altogether independent of the dictionary?

If you were a diamond... if you were a thousand diamonds. Alive. Pulsating, effervescent diamonds - like angels. Embraced by the sun and decorating it making it come very much alive. If you were a thousand queens, of heaven.

I love you,

Shamcher

I send you back this letter too, in addition to the others I sent yesterday... for that book.

January 9, 1976

Dearest Shamcher,

When your letter first came, the impression it gave was from the words that you said - I felt that it's time for me to know more. And there is so much of Sufism that I wish to learn - about a seminar, yet I wonder about it - if this is the way to learning more. I suppose that this is one of the ways.

My concern: there is initiation - and to me it seems a series of continually expanding changes. Each change of viewpoint is a new initiation, yet the big beginning is as the soul takes rightful place in the body, likened to a second birth. This step is a big one. Now from that point I would imagine that, like a baby, the real-self must then develop and mature. Must learn to walk, talk and manipulate things of the world, only the walking and talking are metaphors. What is this growth process? What methods enhance and accelerate it? Is it possible to understand it? I need now to develop further - and I can't say where or what. Perhaps I need to travel to be with many others in a spiritual atmosphere, or perhaps I simply need to wait, to learn patience and watch this atmosphere develop and grow here. The external life I seem to be leading now pains my heart as I drive the car, walk around downtown, buy groceries, and any of the usual activities. I feel myself closing the flower in order to deal with everyday stuff. What I need is to remain always open - the pain is in the closing, not in the influences.

I wish so very much to learn all I can about Sufism, the technology, the ways and means of using the principles of the universe, the various vibrations, etc. I know this is not the goal, and I'd never want just to focus on that. It's the opening, the shining spirit, the star and the continued work that is important. I still feel I need to find more Sufis who know the way from the inside out. Excuse my confusion, I feel so unfocused and jumping about from side to side. Some new change seems to be coming through, and this one is causing a big disturbance. I feel afraid of the change. I write you for reassurance and ask for guideposts; even now I feel remarkably better. Please write to me if you can and somehow I'd appreciate any comments on this letter and the state of mind expressed here.

Love, kisses, tears and love again,

Carol

January 18, 1976

Beloved Carol,

Your letter today better than anything ever, so touchingly touching the basic issues, reasons, loves. During my trip, I harvested the results of our own heavenly relationship, for you have taught me this sublime touch through your heavenly soul.

What do you do now? Exactly what comes to you. A girl at the meet complained of lack of instruction. I responded by quoting how I was thrown into Universal Worship without any instruction at all, then went on to serve in 60 countries; and now in Canada, I said, a girl who has not a fraction of your instruction is equally starting - for these matters are learned direct from God (in your own soul.) And this is the answer. Never be afraid of opening up, but don't show to anyone what your soul does not want to show. Be completely honest, but don't tell what you needn't.

Oh Carol, how I love,

Shamcher

January 19, 1976

Dear Shamcher,

So very much to write you that I hardly know where to begin. Most important surely must be the pack of letters you sent back to me. It just broke my heart and I opened the envelope and saw my own handwriting - I didn't read them then, I read your letter (or felt it - the words were a blur to me) and then with the pack of letters on my lap I cried and cried and cried. How can I even describe my reaction - there are no words, I was so moved, so very very deeply, crying and rocking back and forth. Crying for the entire experience, the years worth of experience and depth of feeling all contained in one package. Afterwards I felt open and so very grateful. The next day I could look at the letters from an entirely different point of view - detached as if they were written by someone else whom I love very much.

I will begin to order them and prepare to somehow have them published along with your replies and your own so splendid letters. How can I thank you for this project? What a remarkable thing you have done by sending me back all which I have poured out to you - I see the process more clearly and in a way you have turned me into my own teacher as I read the letters back to myself. It seems such a beautiful tender document of the process of this love, all written in such a spell of wonder and confusions, the hopes,

105

the heavenly flights are all there - worded.

I wish to tell you so much, yet I feel that all the lists of information would be of little interest - it always changes. And so does the state of my mind and heart. It seems now that more and more horizons are opening, and I'm in entirely uncharted ground. How can I tell if my actions are right or wrong when everything seems to perfectly contain both? Or to say it another way, my entire personality goes through major changes every moment - I seem to be no one at all, ungraspable, and whoever I am with I become so totally seeing the entire world (in and out) through their eyes. I wonder if I should guard myself, for some views are harsh or hurtful yet it happens so naturally and spontaneously - I trust in the guidance and let go. How can I express to you this love for all and everyone, each so separate, yet we are truly one. Agreement, a feeling of joining rather than separation, opens everyone to not feel so alone. In each encounter, to ride with another and to create harmony and a feeling of oneness (in whatever way possible) - this is part of it. Yet as I get swept in the whirls of everyone's life and all, I still must take time to myself, to go within.

People here are so pleased that there is some Sufi activity, and this in turn pleases and encourages me. I'd like this to grow naturally and without pushing, and I wish to learn the balance of organization and spontaneity. I wish to see what this becomes - it is important to create situations where people can just relax entirely all the masks of tension and open up. And within the context of this outer work, there are always my own inner changes which become less and less important.

Let me sing to you how deeply I care for you and let my deepest feelings warm you as a protective and so loving vibration to accompany and heal you always. In my heart you are forever and the cord connecting us is a golden current of love and the true life. Thank you for your being! Some feelings are so very strong - right now is one of the times of just pouring and pouring.

You see I still love you so very very deeply, and the caring broadens, widens, including the entire living breathing universe, the entire creative creation.

Love,
Carol

January 26, 1976

Dear Noble Carol,

Well, perhaps this one seminar on words and music would be good for you and/or Gary. The leader is a sort of genius. But be aware. Aware of what? You'll find out. But come only if convenient for your other duties and your finances. Generally I only go to seminars when I feel some one or more would feel hurt if I didn't. And at the end I promise myself not to go more than strictly necessary. Even at Summerschool with Inayat Khan I felt after the first few days (it lasted 60-90 days) that now I better go home and ponder on the first lesson which is really enough. The constant rush from one concept to another did not feel good to me. Still does not. I see jargon rather than truth, theories, hypothesis rather than fact.

A girl at the last seminar complained she did not have enough instruction to start Universal Worship. Pir Vilayat apologized and yessed. I recalled my primitive initiation (no instruction) after which I performed in 60 countries. I told them about Moineddin's exquisite variations. Because, I said, this is not based on instruction and seminars but on inspiration right from God when and as you need it.

In general, your last letter (which definitely should be included in the book somewhere as a temporary anticlimax) appears weighted by a feeling that you "need to know more". What do you think I know? Nothing at all and that, exactly, is my strength. There is one who knows so much about yoga, talks in a stream for three hours and people swoon. He starts out saying one cannot really talk about yoga. He should have left it at that. He talks about the wheel of reincarnation, lending stupid dogmas to his listeners. Is this what you want to acquire? Your whole mature play (and mine) is just that we don't know - don't know in the sense that we have learned in school to "Know" - know that 2 plus 2 makes 4. Does it? Of course not. You are there, Carol, but you are free to regress into "knowledge" and "seminars" any time you so choose. Sufism or yoga is not knowing but being. My host lady at San Francisco wanted "Darshan" and from me! I looked her in the eyes, deeply. Then I said that I admired what I saw: Courage and Joy. She hugged me frantically. Now she writes me that she had read and heard all about Nirvana, Satori, Samadhi, but never known what it was until WHAM! I gave it all to her in Darshan. Of course, I have none of those things neither do others, but "I" gave it all to her. Now she knows she has it all. You can do the same. What more is there? In what seminar? The world is yours, as long as you know you don't know. You cannot know. My hostess said, "I went to Pir's seminar, my body went, but my consciousness was in my forehead - where you, Shamcher, had touched." It is she not me. It is your pupil, not you. God is in Edmonton. Not any more at the Seminar. But go when you want to.

LOVE

Shamcher

P.S. You need less and less to close. You will be able to stand the pain from all the "jarring" influences hitting your open heart. Indeed they won't be "jarring" anymore. You know their nature, their divinity.

January 27, 1976

Dear dear Shamcher,

Oh how very heartening to hear from you in the way you sent me that lovely packet of beautiful letters, and your own dear letter best of all. The whole package encourages me so very much, and through it all came the beautiful realization of what the new Sufism is all about - a vision so very deep and remarkable that I can barely express it in words. Suffice it to say that I am now completely confident that the work I am doing here and wherever else I am led, is absolutely right in focus and aim - just essential love, humility and service - the work being the annihilation of the ego and total surrender to God - that through each being the One can truly manifest. All the practices, all that stuff comes naturally when needed; God provides, in forms I cannot even dream of. And Sufism in the West will come into adolescence (I won't say maturity, for there is a long way to go. Yet for sure the end of childhood is upon us.) Oh, certainly doubts will arise, foolishness will try to get in the way, yet the light forever shines, and inside each of us is the only place to ever find it.

Oh Shamcher, I can see it all so clearly, surely this will occur. It is already occurring on a small scale through us, yet it will grow at an astonishing rate - the simple transmission of love flowing through all. It is the self-trust, the absolute trust in the eternal self which will call this one to flower and grow within. Oh Shamcher, somehow I don't seem to care at all that I don't know a thing about Sufi practices or all the rituals, these will come. The essence shines brilliant in love's own light which is itself shine, brilliancy, love, light, being, oneness, all. (Yet I don't deny practices and welcome any chance to learn more in all ways.)

Wouldn't it be good to see one another? I'd love to give you a big hug, share time with you (this time I wouldn't get sick!) So much I'd love to hear from you, all sorts of things we should discuss. My love for you is beyond the being of "me" and "you" for this love *is* by the giving of "me" and "you" to form its life - the true life.

Why do I keep writing and wording the unwordable? It is a passion. Let me just say thank you, thank you, diamond-star-being - I am with you this instant in love forever.

Love,

Carol

P.S. Now all these lovely women are falling in love with you, you'll have to become as Krishna with the gopis! I have no words for this marvelous peace filling my being since receiving your letter. I send it all back to you to fill your already overflowing cup.

January 30, 1976

Carol! ! ! ! ! !

Here are three fabulous letters again. When you sit looking and knowing another person's soul and suddenly see and are occupied by some-thing else, that you aren't tied to and by the first experience - is an excellent sign that you are unattached, the very essence of spiritual maturity. Absorbed but not attached. So you can be and are free at any moment to forget and switch to what is more needed at that moment. It also shows that you can never be disappointed. For if the other fellow, or lady, also shifts, you don't resent. You know that it is also your way.

Love,

Shamcher

January 30, 1976

Dear Beloved Hidayat,

Your beautiful letter with the inspired words on Visalat Day reminds me of that day of February 5, 1927, when a flock of us gathered at Fazal Manzil guided by a not yet fully developed sense. We came from Holland, France, England, and even as far away as Sweden and Norway. I had packed a little bag and embarked on a ship, not yet knowing why. My senses were in control, yet I did not follow them, or any reason. I just up and went. I had no premonition, not even any idea why I went or for what. I arrived in Suresnes on the fifth of February and found many others there, though not all, not the usual crowd of the Summer School. Then came the message, Oh yes, that is why we had come. Now we knew. And you were there, and Noor, and her sister and Vilayat. Now it was us. The heavy burden of the message was now on us, with us. This day was the mightiest initiation. Visalat Day.

Dear Hidayat, in your last letters you have called me "murshid." Why? Some years ago Pir Vilayat asked me if I would serve as "general representative" because they needed such a bird and there was no one else. "On one condition," I said, "No title." A few years later. Pir Vilayat made some people murshid and told them I had already been one for a long time - possibly so not to give the new "murshids" the idea they were "higher" than an old mureed of Pir-O-Murshid. But I extracted the promise of all I talked to that they would never use this title on me. It set me off as something special. You, Hidayat, have the right to call me whatever you like, you alone. But the name Pir-O-Murshid gave me was Shamcher. It is enough.

Love,

Shamcher

January 30, 1976

Dear Shamcher,

Rolls and rolls of loving waves of deep feelings of tenderness, like clouds before a rain all gathering over you to shower kisses! and stars!

Love,

Carol

August 12, 1975

Dear ____,

....All titles or hierarchies expressed in this world, while pretending to be functions, are not true functions but dilettantic games. You have a very good mind. Why do you still worry about these things?

Now as to direct communication: That happens in a world for which the language we use, such as English, French, or Arab or Russian - has no words. Therefore any explanation would be entirely faulty. I knew, not always but often, people's feelings or thoughts when I was a child. I could communicate directly with Inayat Khan at age 26-29 but not with others at that time. By simple meditations I gradually regained lost talents - though not until I was in the seventies. Patient meditation did it. Often you write to me about your feelings and views that I already know. But it seems to me you are more angry with me than you express in your gracious letters. Your ideas on this would be appreciated.

Can I teach you to thus communicate? No, and I believe nobody can. But I can tell you how I achieved a half-way ability and you might try the same: Meditation at definite hours each day. For example from 4:20 a.m. on in the morning. That suits me. And the breathing I taught you before that, in fresh air. Now, what kind of meditation? For you I would think: No object: no person, no picture but simply void your mind of appetites - for food, sex, possessions, progress, money, wealth, fame. In the emptiness a third part of yourself peeps forth: Intuition. After many or few years. After months or centuries. That is all I can say.

There are psychics. They are called, in my book, distorted. They tell you they can predict events with 80% accuracy. Phooey on them. God has not even decided on those issues and they try to rob God of his options. So many astrologers do the same. You may call the psychic talents "gifts." Mostly they are gifts produced by a misdirected urge, another appetite. An appetite for being different, able to do what most others cannot do. Not bad in itself, perhaps, but bad when predicting happenings - instead of creating those happenings by our actions.

Not merely mystics but doctors, economists, senators play the stupid game of forecasts. Forecasts become excuses for inaction. They are based on past follies rather than the future we should create. In that sense psychics are undesirable. You may reach a stage where you see patterns, but you know or should know that these patterns may not necessarily occur. You try to change what ought to be changed, rather than advertising your wonderful sixth or fourteenth sense.

Love,

Shamcher

August 26, 1975

Dear _____,

That which you call your frustration and which I termed with some reckless abandon anger is your asset, showing that you are not entrapped, so be secure and be assured that you are not buying the glitter.

No, a good mind does not mean a good intellect. The intellect is only a minor part of the mind. A good mind means a mind basically able to develop into the next stage: Intuition. But intuition may develop with a less

than good mind too.
Love,
Shamcher

February 6, 1976

Dear dear Carol,

Beautiful letter - you are so right that all arguments, all opinions resolve in the fire and flames of love.

You should be open to all, of any type, but not in the sense that all your power goes freely to them. You should not be open for all their influences on you. You should listen sufficiently to keep in touch, yes, but when unholy emotions will press themselves upon you, be detached, pleasant, but not accepting them. Or you will be crushed. You can do that. No "technique" has to be learned. In fact, techniques may harm and divert.
Love,
Shamcher

February 6, 1976

Dear Shamcher,

Your letter full of advice and wisdom telling me to let go all that foolishness came to reinforce what had already gone on within. Part of the reason why I "regressed" is that I am pregnant! So I'm back to square one dealing with deep emotions and tendencies which I thought were gone forever - here they all rise up again - little insecurities and conservative selfishness. So it is a whole new self to work with and an entirely new personality - a new everchanging emotional range. At the time I wrote that letter I wasn't aware of my condition. We are both ecstatic and look forward with great anticipation.

Last night at Sufi meeting we had silence which was most beautiful. It was as if the whole room just changed gears into another level. Everyone felt the uselessness of talk, everyone felt the beauty of silence - then we sang, had tea and broke up - everyone that night changed slightly. All this happened through us all - the spirit moved through the group. And this is just a beginning. I am taken in wonder at the marvelous process at work. Many people want to dance, and I say yes, we should, it would be good and fun. What I feel is that essential Sufism exists here now forever, in all, through all, in each moment of everyday life.

This world is a beautiful being radiant in the morning pulsating in love. Light shines through us all to show the way. So much pours through me to you - and through you to me - golden lines between us.

Isn't it amazing that I am having a baby? I feel so strongly this new soul coming.

Lots of love,

Carol

February 8, 1976

Dear dear Carol,

Why I enclose copies of these two letters I don't really know. Perhaps to share with you my wonder. Also to tell you all this wonder came without even a kiss. Hugs, yes, but even that seemed not necessary, should perhaps not have been. Yet, something is stirring in my mind that perhaps should not be stirring. Or should be stirring for the last time. And I wonder how I would do in the future. One of these is 50, the other 23 and delicately beautiful.

Have you taught me or us all this? Was that how it was opened up? Yet, in the way of the universe it is so common, so trite in a way, "Everybody knows it." Do they? They should. It would change the economy, ecology, the working places.

Carol, you are so precious, having caused all this, having lifted me up, swung me over the barrier, made me see God, made me be God. Aren't you a miracle?

Of course.

Penetrating love, overriding me. Will you protect me so I always choose rightly? Do the right things?

Oh thank you Carol - you queen of my soul,

Shamcher

February 9, 1976

Dear dear dear Carol and who else,

What exciting good news that you shall guide another soul across the threshold. She/he will have a lucky star in being in you and all the wonder that you are now. What a start for a coming soul. It is stupendous. I know you will be careful and that we all must be careful about the emotions and thoughts now allowed to enter and whirl around in your brilliant mind and sensitive heart.

Just for your information: the old Inayat Khan Gatha Classes went like this: Two, three minutes silence after reading *Toward the One, the perfection of...* (and so on.) Then reading three, four or five gathas. Then say the three prayers with movements. Then go home quietly. No discussion. Some may like that. Others may like it differently. Some may like both, but a different time. The gathas have a sacred effect. To talk about them sometimes destroys that effect. The leader's comments may not be the same as the participants. He tears down something in them. You may have discussion some other evening. Some may come to both, some to only one of the evenings .... silent gatha readings or the discussion evenings. Instead of gathas you may read chapters of the books. Generally do whatever you like, or let things develop before you, doing nothing.

Yes, golden lines --------------- LOVE

Shamcher

February 24, 1976

Dear Shamcher,

I'm getting the letters together in some form or other, what a task it is! Several of the difficulties are in the ordering - do I put them in the order they were written or do I put them in a way that one can see the responses one to the other? Sometimes the chronological order doesn't really work, but the criss-crossed mailing makes the other way difficult to understand, too. So I just keep on reading them and hoping to get them into some form that has continuity. Reading and working with the letters is a beautiful experience but certainly takes a lot out of me each time I sit down with them. It is so intense that I can only work in short spurts, then become exhausted emotionally. I don't need to tell you just how deeply I feel your presence in this work. Please write soon, or better yet, arrive.

All my love,

Carol

February 25, 1976

Dearest Shamcher,

Why do I keep on writing to you when almost every letter I send to you is sent back to me - all the feelings and devotions sent right back!!

Oh, Shamcher, I feel more and more strongly that I must see you. Yet right now I am on the bed and staying for the week to come - the doctor tells me there is a chance of miscarriage - so I'm resting and keeping my feet up. I am confident that this rest and staying in without changing rhythm will save this baby. I'm not sure if this pregnancy will prove stable enough to withstand much travel. We'll see as time goes on. Certainly we must see one another soon.

How wonderfully the sufi meetings develop and grow. People are becoming warmer and more open, there is less and less need to talk. We sing a lot and the group is getting closer. Each meeting the rhythm is different, each time it is deeper and easier.

How can we see each other? Is it too much to ask you to come here for a short time? So many people wish you to see them but I have this strong urge to be near you for a time - to sunbathe in your warm sun and to tenderly hold your hand, to gaze into your eyes and with my voice to say to you "I love you" warmly. Such tender feelings. Also - to be with you past tender feelings in a somewhat deeper realm.

You know, I have all the letters which you have ever written to me, saved from the beginning, all except one which was in my pocket one day and was lost. Can you send me a copy? It was a reply to the letter you just sent back. I wrote that I wanted to give everything up and certainly didn't want to organize sufis, and you wrote back that I must and why and how, etc. It was a good letter and if you could find a copy of it I'd really appreciate it.

I must somehow increase my physical strength. This feeling of weakness is strange to me - so easily fatigued. Yet with a short rest I am back to normal - so many changes - the beauty of life.

Love,

Carol

February 27, 1976

Dear Carol,

So exciting to have another letter from you. Yes, Inayat Khan and his cousin Ali used breath. Inayat for everything, Ali especially for healing. He would breathe on his fingers, hand held (right hand) with thumb toward mouth and nose, then as he breathed, he would cut the hand like an axe toward the sick limb or point. It comes natural when you have done much regular breathing. Inayat Khan never did this. You had a feeling he synchronized his breath with you when he communicated. As to myself, I don't think of breath when I communicate. But I have the feeling that when contact is likely, for being established by love and insight and moral purity, breath takes its line, smoothes itself to your requirements. No technique, no separate effort or arrangement is involved in this for me. I sometimes wonder if those who use technique do not thereby limit themselves to technology. I think I see many "professionals" who thus limit themselves, lacking the deeper reality.

Love,

Shamcher

P.S. Such a workshop might be all right. But don't accept him if he requires money plus travel expenses. Just say you'll have him later on when you can afford it. Or do your members want to pay out a lot of money? Mostly that is the beginning of the end. Members say, "Okay, since they asked this time I'll pay but I better get out of this expensive business."

February 27, 1976

Dear Shamcher

You are a fountain, continually overflowing. Another letter came today, with the revision and the letters. Your whole letter was most amazing to me and the energy in it just picked me up and carried me away - out of the constant concern about my body and into the real realms where we dwell!! I am still lifted out of the worries, etc. which can too easily fog me over in pregnancy.

The sufi work, inner and outer, is alive and true to me - all sorts of energy for this. And seeing people - all sorts of energy for that. Writing to you - of course. Yet nothing else draws my attention but that and this baby. (Oh bodily and emotional changes!) So I must work on the insecurities which come in - where and why? I am so very sure in my faith and trust - yet clouds still get in the way. My work has begun all over again. When I'm overwhelmed by feelings of dependency, I shift the dependence from whomever, whatever, to God and depend firmly on the real. What an incredible test this one is!

All your letters have been a great comfort to me - all we have shared and continue to work within and play within surrounds me in a very helpful vibration. Our connection gives a strength I can always draw upon. I have been feeling as if I'm drawing all the energies of the universe into myself to create this new being's home. This is a time when I am taking in more than giving out. It's like one big in-breath right now!

And so my dearest, I trust you'll bear with me if I may pull a little on you. My work seems monumental in this time, to control appetites, reactions, thoughts, etc. It's natural that these changes occur and I ride them as best as I can. It's wide swings of emotion which I find most difficult. I haven't felt such anger or frustrations or possessiveness in years. This emotional climate is what I must control. I say *Ya Rafa Ya Dafa* (from the time you gave it to me) and trust there is help in this.

Please know that in this storm I feel more than ever a dedication to clearly sword my way through all confusions - cutting swiftly all the brambles growing up around the heart. Part of it is a natural protection, maternal instincts, but I can't let it carry on into selfishness and such. This, too, will change.

I love you deeply, dearly, strongly, tenderly, beyond all.

Carol

Undated

Dear J___,

Yes, from as early as I can remember I seem to have known (what is "known" anyway?) that there was something before and something after, but as a separate personality? Why, we aren't separate even here, less and less the more I see. But somewhat separate, in some respects, changing respects.

But nothing can be transferred from one consciousness to another. Thoughts yes, but convictions or "beliefs," no. I used to say: I believe in nothing, disbelieve in nothing.

One may start out with two questions: Is it really important to have a "theory"? I'd say for some (such as me) better not. I really don't care whether I "survive" or not, though all evidence I can see points to survival, including my own experiences at different times. Second question: What survives? If anything? Mainly mind. That goes on with bang until death and cannot cease then. Some, with little mind, sleep through the death period and come back never recalling that there was something before. People with minds survive very much, but is it they, the souls that survive or just the mind matter? Inayat Khan thinks the soul only comes here once and brings with it a melee of mind matter, and there may be such a logical sequence in the mind matters brought along by different souls that the half-ignorant see it as the same life coming again and again. I do not know if this is exactly right nor what it exactly means but I do know, or feel, that there is survival of mind matter.

So what? I keep open house. The less I dogmatize about it the better I feel and the better chance I have of adjusting and even finding out a few truths. But it is certainly not a very big difference when we go to "the other side" (and how many other sides?) We continue to be ignorant and long for theories (of that which we longed for before.)

No doubt each person has his own distinct survival. experience, so general theories are useless, false.

Highest regards,

Bryn

February 28, 1976

Dear Carol,

It was so good to hear your voice again. Enclosed are some of your most unique and tremendously useful letters again, as it portrays with such feeling and such skill the fluctuations of a woman in such a situation as you are now. I don't know if any of the other letters enclosed is the one you asked for. And . . . perhaps we shall meet and see each other next Saturday.

Love,

Shamcher

March 1, 1976

Dear Shamcher,

It seems like ages since I last heard from you and how I have been looking forward to receiving a letter or a phone call or some word. Much that I really need to discuss with you, yet a letter is not appropriate for this - and also to tell you of the events of the past while.

We began Gatha classes last week and my goodness, what a different energy. To me it was something I had never felt in such a way before. At one point, I was reading and what I was saying flowed out, but you know, it wasn't what was written on the page. Yet it was true and right. This was only for a few words. It was difficult for me to remain here - an inexpressible feeling. I don't feel frightened, but it is so very unfamiliar. When it was over I was gone from the rest of the world for a time, everything went on around me but I felt almost as if I had disappeared and wasn't there at all. I feel that once it is more familiar to me to be in these realms, then the energy will flow more freely. Beautiful.

I am going to be doing a radio program in a few months. It will be a weekly half-hour of music and readings from the various religious traditions; whatever recordings are available will be interspersed with readings. We will emphasize the oneness of the traditions, and I'm certain that many people will really enjoy it.

The letters are now in an order, but dear me, there are many of my letters to you which are missing. There is a span of months where I have many letters from you to me but none the other way. It is only for continuity's sake that I wish to include them.

I'm so encouraged, for I've seen in reading the letters that when I was most on the edge, most unsure of what was happening - that was when I was most real and closest to the truth. Working with the letters makes me feel so close to you and to wish to be near you to discuss certain parts with you and share some of the understandings that come. And so I spontaneously do, for I feel closer to you now than ever before. Truly as close as to say you are my own self, or I am your self, the channel seems so clear that I can call upon you any time and feel your presence. When I feel love for you I know it is sent and received in the simultaneous instant.

Truly there are no barriers to any communication or contact, and no barriers to love which fills this whole universe with the beauty of being. In the way I feel close to you, I also feel close to Inayat Khan, and any time I can call upon him for aid, and to share with, or to give to, or for strength. And of course, the connection to God for aid and strength and to humbly thank for the beauty and to be one and to be all is a marvel of the love which we all are. To send you this is just to wave out these deep very fine feelings and to expand from this limited little self to existence, one more exquisite breath.
Much love,
Carol

November 18, 1975

Dear D__,

You flattered me but also made me feel humble and unable when you told that you had planned to meditate at the same absolute time as I. What could I have done for you? I am not a teacher. Wonder if anyone is. The other things you say brings to mind how each one of us is encapsuled in a protective shroud through which no one can see - or can some? In that case, how? when?

Your trouble with "God" seems to come from loyalty to teachers and teachings. I never had that. From birth on I did not accept any church. Didn't offend them either. My mother and father were likewise, even though my mother was of a family of clerics. She showed respect but had no faith in them. "God" in my childhood was a good playmate with lots of fun. Later I found him inside myself - and in you. But when you predict a future of no energy, you are making the God in you a bit too narrow. For me, I know my duty to be to give all my energy to develop sensible patterns for the whole, and God and me (God in me) do not always succeed but we work on that assumption that we do. For God - the All - is not at all perfect or omnipotent at this time. We limit him by time patterns. In the overall timeless space-time he and we are all-powerful. In a limited time - one.

Whenever I say the morning prayer (Through the rays of the sun, through the waves of the air...) sweet energy flows through my veins, nerves, a direct response from whatever some call God. Why should he uglify life by replying in rigid words? What are words anyway? Words are your own creation and may be inspired from God but are not his words. We live by and with structures. Everybody constructs rigid concepts. They want "God" to come down and be embedded in some of these stupid concepts. So he does not even burp. It is not a matter of "faith". What is faith? Often stupid structures. People listen to a preacher then go home to try out his willy-nilly theories. Can you live without words? No reading or writing? Not even knowing how, perhaps? I have met people who could neither read nor write, in any language, yet knew God. Can you not know him if you can read or write? Of course, though not through reading or writing. That would be unfair, to illiterates at least. "True wisdom is not found in any book," say the Chinese - then flood us with books, about I Ching, Acupuncture, Buddhism, Confucius, Lao Tze.

You are right in getting a farm and living. You are not right in thinking or even predicting that this will be the only survival or that the society as we know it will collapse. By so thinking you are one of the small causes to make it happen. Alone, you are not all-powerful, particularly not at this time - or any limited time.

Cheer up. "Oh Lord, liberate me from all the obscuring veils, allurements, and chains of attachment." This is the cry of the seeker after truth.

Love,

Shamcher

March 5, 1976

Dear Carol,

Your enclosed letter was both a flattery and a criticism. Flattery because you indicate you'd have liked to hear from me oftener, critical because I didn't write often enough. It must be the post offices. I've written almost every day, being embarrassed thinking you'd be tired of my missiles (I mean missives.)

Yes, wouldn't I love just to fly right up and see you? But I have to go through a long process of purification and refinement before I am worthy to meet that great Canadian stock of the noble British vein - me, a poor simple American or should I say USA man, a mixture of all and any races, Polish, Romanian, Hindu, Japanese, Chinese - even plain Norwegians! And one who has even discarded his good old Norwegian name and adopted a mongrel moniker that no one in this whole world shares for its lowness and simplicity. Now in addition you may have told your people up there that I am up to ordinary standards, so how could I show myself in my gruesome simplicity and ignorance? It will be such a letdown.

I am thrilled about the Gatha classes, excellent stuff for the letter-book.

Portland? I told you all about Portland. It was really quite exciting. I was talking a lot, I talked a lot, perhaps too much, but how could I refuse? There is a communication - and I learned it from you, wonderful super-earthy you you you - remember? That is it. You have a wonderful group there now under your sublime leadership. Why should I come and disturb that? Oh say that you want me to come anyway, I need to hear that, but should I, really? You know, beautiful Carol, you are way ahead of me. You light and burn with a colossal flame. I am like a moth in it. But please be very careful, constantly. Your light is so bright it tempts desperately and - have you always showed that you master your surroundings? Have you?

The radio program sounds completely sufi, and wonderful. Yes, true, there is the presence, always, including Inayat Khan and all.
Love, hugs, kisses if I am allowed, your slave,
Shamcher

March 5, 1976

Dearest Shamcher,

Hello! This letter is to tell you how very grateful I am to you - for you have actually pointed me in the right direction. I feel so sure of this, with all the

121

whirling around, the New Ageness of all the pyramids, astrology, numerology, etc. All of them work to some degree, but how do they intrinsically help one out of the mess? More and more I wish for just simplicity and natural being - love opens all doors. There is no surer way, no safer way than to fall into the arms of love and thereby be forever guided by God, nature, all light shining within. Oh and sharing this shining - seeing all beings gloriously shining this same one. And I have one true lover - who is seen shining through each person, all things aglow. Through you, then, this one showed himself/itself/herself to him/it/herself in me - yet no you and me just this one in love recognition - this! The way reveals itself all within and without at the same time! So thank you dear you for guiding me straight to the heart, without all the fuss and rigamarole in between. There is no need for externals, the fountain within is never-ending.

Love,

Carol

This letter remained unmailed, and now I add to it some of my incredible sadness and confusion of last night. In my deep tears my only thought was Shamcher please come and help me and this was burning very deep. So sincerely and deeply I ask you with all my heart to please, if in any way you can come to see me, now is a time when I need you. The waves in the air last night were no doubt felt by you - I have never had such deep confusion - except perhaps in San Anselmo. And this seems to occur in a place in my heart which has only been touched by you.

More and more clearly a picture of my work here is becoming focused. I can see that this way of no rigid hierarchical framework is very difficult for most people to accept. Only a few actually see, and this, only glimpses. Those who see, do; and those who don't, can't. The spontaneous flow occurs without anything to do with me, my wishes, etc. It is this work which shows the way of humility.

Thank you for your being, for the kindness you are and the strength. And thank you for pointing me to this path which is surely a more difficult way than any other - with only God to rely on and intuition to guide - the sign posts are often hidden. This way is most natural to me and is most true. Yet more difficult than following prescribed grades and stages and all. Without absolute faith and trust, I'd be lost. Without the conviction in my heart there would be nothing. I trust this way over and over, and my tears last night were for that.

March 6, 1976

Carol!

Your last letter - jewel upon iewel upon jewel upon diamonds upon suns upon sheer beauty. Beauty is the only worship-deserving. And your name! In ancient Egypt the KA, the first syllable of your name, is the real hidden person, often wandering about by itself, more often acting upon the outside self from the inside (not all Egyptians were very good at understanding - most of them not as good as you or I, but some of them were.) And your KA (CA) rolls with the punches, accepts life and rolls with it into new life and into ever more beauty, ever more truth (for isn't truth beauty and beauty truth?)

You are so right, so right, so right, in everything you say in this letter and in previous letters.

Portland? Well a girl there had embarrassed me by asking to be my "mureed" so I had to go down to tell her that I would be honored to be her mureed and this pleased her so much that she hugged me, and then the other five girls in that lovely house got the idea and we had a hugging feast, first one at a time then two then three then all five interhugging in one big multihug. Now, Carol, what kind of nonsense is this? Oh, it is not nonsense really for I learned all this from you though in a different way. I would not have known how to answer these girls and know what to do if it hadn't been for you. Every one of them insisted on crowding into the car to say goodbye at the railroad station. One of them hugged me even there, I had to promise to come back as soon as possible.

Carol, comparing with your exquisite letters, am I not a fool to write you all this rot? But then it may please you to see the difference and your own superiority. I also talked too much to those girls, and some times didn't talk at all, just stood and looked.

Carol here it is: love,

Shamcher

March 11, 1976

My dear Carol,

From your last two letters (in one envelope) it is clear that I must come soon. At present I cannot talk, something in my talk box, and others may come from time to time, of course you cried and crying washes away your self, so now you are ready to act.

Once a wild-looking sufi sheikh came from Algeria to Inayat Khan's summer school in Suresnes. We had the feeling he would command his hordes to slay us if our sufism was not exactly as he thought it ought to be. Inayat Khan humbly bowed to him and said we were just having a tiny little group here, studying the ancient wisdom of the sufis. He blessed us forcefully and left without having us slayed.

Love, my wonderful Carol, love,

Shamcher

Please also tell your flock that one of the great things with Inayat's sufi message was women's equalization with men, women even higher (in man we designed our image, in woman we completed it) Women cherags, women murshidas (teachers.)

March 23, 1976

Beloved and lovely Carol,

I haven't heard from you for so long and all the wonderful things you have sent me through the air have not yet wiped away my anxiety. What's wrong with me? We should be so thoroughly entwined, words should not be necessary anymore. But still I need them, I am crying for them - just a few at least.

Carol, all sufis, all teachers, experience the same, most of them at a certain point lose all their disciples. But they stand up to the Lord who is omniscient and most merciful and thank him, thank him for all that was and the best that is; and they come back. For there is no work wasted. But many people on the path waver and whimse. So let them. There is only one path. When they leave, you have time to do your other work - ready to work with them again when they return, after one year or a thousand. But all this talk - what for? There is, maybe, something else. Maybe a letter for me tomorrow?

Love and longing,

Shamcher

P.S. The weekend April 10-11 seems now best, for if desired, I could stay a day or two beyond the strict weekend. Say, do you have a fairly good dentist? How does he charge? Now tell me frankly if you just as well wish I don't come.

March 21, 1976

Dear Shamcher,

Happy spring! It seems like ages since I have written you forgive me for it - last week I was sort of in the doldrums, and all my energy was going into just maintaining things here.

This pregnancy is now past the three months stage, and part of the lessened activity of last week was due to this change of rhythm. The changes come so fast and so deep, one day I am full of energy and the next day I am just drawing it all in toward me, in and out.

I am so eagerly waiting to hear from you as to when you could come for a while, even a day would be such a blessing and fine feeling - not only for me but for this new child. Nothing would please me more than for her/him to spend a short time in your beautiful influence.

It's hard for me to word this letter as I haven't been in the rhythm of writing for a week or more and the words don't flow as easily.

I appreciate your dear letters more than I can possibly express and look forward to hearing a word from you whenever you have the time. Your being is strong within me and there is little else to say except that I am with you now in love and this will be so forever. Please be well and remember that I dwell within your heart (I have so secretly placed myself there like a stowaway elf,) and from this place there fountains eternally innumerable blessings of all sorts, radiating in all directions. And of course this has nothing to do with either you or me, it is our very self.

All love and all joy on this fine spring day,
Carol

March 22, 1976

My dearest Shamcher,

Your letter was so touching and beautiful that I really have no words to send, only great round sparkling thoughts and deep waves of feeling. Oh, how I look so very much forward to seeing dear beautiful you again - oh so much to tell you that there is nothing to say.

This baby is growing inside me and I have splendid baby dreams almost every night. What a blessing this whole experience is!

You know Shamcher, that it is you who showed me the way and continue to do so, you ...who are you? Who am I? The caring we share never ever ends for it is our being - whole and beautiful. Great feelings fill the air

125

towards you as I think of and feel your deep being. It seems to me that I see you clearly now, in the way our work/play is one. So often I simply don't know what I am doing, or what is best, yet I follow that unseen unknown unspeaking little voice that miraculously leads to the right thing at the right time. To clearly hear (unhear?) this little unvoice - oh so much I cannot say.

But I can say I love you deeply and tenderly in all ways even beyond what I consider to be my capacity for giving and yours for receiving. You know, often when I write it seems not to be me at all but truly the voice of Inayat Khan - and also others, yet mainly this one guiding light. Often when I say "I love you" there is a depth beyond what the words write.

Must go,

Love,

Carol

April 5, 1976

Carol, my dear,

Two fabulous letters from you, right back now. It seems you must try to reproduce in the book all the wonderful pictures - this star, the star flowers, all.

I have made a reservation for Saturday April 10 and should arrive at Edmonton airport at 4:50 by flight no: 228 Canadian airlines.

So lucky that I just had a two hours talk with Hidayat yesterday which I can convey to you. I asked him to come along to Edmonton and he said yes he hoped some day but he couldn't now. And now I have so much to say - about your feelings going beyond your capacity for giving - or mine - such beautiful but above all TRUE things that you say that - I just have to get this in the mail before it is too late. . .

Love,

Shamcher

April 14, 1976

Fantastic beloved Carol,

No thanks would do, not even four billion. So just ... Thank you, thank you Carol, Gary, cats, Bill, Diane, Tony, Ahmed, Lory, all. . .

Also enclosed is a letter to Pir Vilayat and the sufi secretary Sikander.

Oh, Carol, you are all so glorious.

Shamcher

April 15, 1976

Dear Shamcher,

Thank you so much for your beautiful visit. It was marvelous to be with you again - I feel more inspired and in some way more sure of following my own intuition than ever before.

As to all the other situations, I don't really care! Whatever happens I'll just work within it in my own way. Today you are back at work and I am here feeling so close to you that there is no separation despite the idea of distance, time.

Truly we are one and if I could shine back to you even a small part of your own shining it would rebound off all the stars!

I hope you weren't too tired of all that running around and I trust all is well at home for you. I love you on all planes at and in every imaginable world and way. Thank you for the great gift of your being here for those few days.

And what a wake you left behind you!

Forever,

Carol

April 20, 1976

Dearest Shamcher,

Now I feel the resonances from your visit in me and I see it in others. For myself there seems to be a new vista and new way. I might seem the same to the outside, but within I feel a greater dedication and I've come to see that I simply cannot allow lesser attributes of my personality to stand in the way of effective action. I've been holding back and not working at my full potential. The strength I now feel is not the totality, but it is what I can handle at this time. How remarkable - I never expected this at all! It took a while to seep through, but once it did I felt so very freed from whatever those old habits were.

Oh Shamcher what can I send you in a letter and even when we are together, how can I show you how I love you? How is it possible to express this love here? How can it shine through all the limits and beyond?

As to the other situation, if I deal rightly in this then it will be a good lesson indeed. And I feel I can choose just how much I will learn through this - I can go part way and learn part of it. But if I can maintain harmony and at the same time make the best of the situation, by this I mean turn it into a

127

greater change, then it will be complete.

Such abstractions. I hope some of this is clear to you. Frankly I don't know who or what I am or what I am doing. Yet I so totally trust and hope to act quickly and rightly when it's needed in every situation and time -
Enough of this writing, I so look forward to hearing from you.
Love love love,
Carol

April 21, 1976

Inscrutible, infallible, beloved Carol,

Where did I fail? Why hast thou forsaken me? I know I am impossible. You must tell me how to get up and out and improve. I had a piece they had asked, begged for in *The Message*. They didn't take it. It is about *The Art of Learning*. I cannot even find a copy. When I find one I shall send you. (You can tell me why it failed.) My friend of whom you have seen earlier correspondence, is hungering for a farm. I have no idea whether you would like him or he Canada. I just wrote him enclosed letter.

Oh Carol, how I worry when I don't hear from you. Or are you busy finding your farm and publishing that book? Or soothing our good Achmed? You promised me his address, remember?
Your glow is still with me from Edmonton.
Love,
Shamcher
P.S. Be sure to tell me that you have inserted these new chapters 1, 2 & 3 in *Planet Earth* and thrown away the old 1, 2 & 3.

April 21, 1976

Dear Shamcher,

Here I am again more confused than ever! It seems that some change is going on. I'm sort of lost and don't really know anything anymore. I'm not sure of my concepts of what's what and there seems nothing to replace them. I alternate between being afraid and just letting go. When I woke up this morning my first thought was to write you.

I look back at the past months when I felt so "sure" and they seem less alive than now when I feel "unsure." This is the right working of it all, but still the fears, etc. cause confusion. How is it possible to work on oneself and at the same time be all involved in organization? What I really mean to say is not that at all. For the world I used to know is disintegrating before me like melting snow. It is so terrifying to "little me" though "big me" is so pleased. Part of me wants the process to accelerate and really explode - the other part of me can't even handle the present changes.

What to do? How can I calm myself to ride through this gracefully? Why don't I allow the real to manifest more often? Because it is so deep, so much deeper than ever before, yet more smooth and easier. What am I saying? And why am I writing this to you? I can't say just what it is that I'm alluding to through these words. I hope that the thought comes through as it is. I feel open and exposed yet very safe - all confusion and paradox. Help, she called.

Love,

Carol, what is happening? who am I?

April 23, 1976

Dear Carol,

As to your recent doubts - you have a greater load than I, for I have such a great comforter, who always turns me in the right direction when I waver. Her name is Carol. But you have no great Carol to help you in such a situation, for you are Carol herself, and you have only little Shamcher.

Yes yes Carol, I am just like you, up and down, up and down, all the time. But I laugh at it - both up and down I laugh, laugh happily. No sting anymore. Observation.

Love,

Little Shamcher

April 23, 1976

Carol!!!

Here came your message, a healing breeze, bringing everything into focus and sense again - and you know what? You had written that blessed message on Wednesday, the day after I had left and it reached me nine days later. Nine days! Like in the old days with horse-teams.

Maybe we should go back to horses. As Hu Feng, the horse trader of Chinghai told me in 1950 when I suggested airplanes were good for moving somewhere.

"We have horses for that!" he brusquely informed me.

Thank you Carol, love,

Shamcher

My friend who said I was "the esoteric head of the world" says "Bryn" is a clear sound that keeps his mind operating, while "Shamcher" cracks the mind apart though his soul flows high. With me it is Carol.

April 27, 1976

Dear Shamcher,

Thank you so much for all you've sent to me in the past few days, the letters and the phone call and of course just all the support which I do feel coming so beautifully through the air always. Sometimes I may be too cloudy to feel it, I am still forever reassured and comforted to know that you are there, shining.

These past times have been very busy and I feel in a new rhythm once again. It is enjoyable to rest well in the rest times and work well in the work times. I begin teaching meditation classes tonight, and though I can't really say what I can possibly contribute, I will go and help where I can. The same with everything I do, I just don't know where it is going or what I must do in it all, so I just carry on and continue. Life is certainly beautiful. I'm enjoying the development of the little one inside me so much, all the new feelings and the growing, the actual growing of a new being inside me!

Your last letters have shown me something new, something I can't really express but it warms me to think of you and to feel you so deeply. To think of you or to speak of you lightens me, in a way, and all becomes shimmery for a time. Since your visit I've found that I more readily trust my intuition and follow what the little inner voice tells me, even if it seems to me to be a little nutty or perhaps without too much purpose. This has led me to some good situations, and some fine deep contacts with people. Not that I just plunge headlong into everything, but I wait, and if it remains insistent, then I act without another thought. Sometimes I could make an error, but I must follow my heart to learn what comes next.

Forever with you,

Carol

May 1, 1976

Dear Shamcher,

At last there is time to sit down, catch my breath and write to you who have been on my mind and in my heart so much these past days. Why is it that we are so connected that even across the miles, with only a few times of seeing each other and by letter and phone, we are together like forever many-lifetime companions - deeply and strongly together as one.

I have a question which is cropping up from time to time. I let things ride to listen to what should be done, yet often I am torn - it seems I can't really help anybody much at all. Perhaps through contact there is a shared space of exhilaration or calm or whatever you could describe, of deep communication - love - yet basically there is little change and the same old habits and ways still continue to drive the personality away from the truth. And I see this and it saddens me. Is it that I don't do all I can? Is it that it is best not to interfere? Right now I hold back from saying anything direct. I feel I can do nothing to help people. Of course this includes me as well - I slide back and forth, open and closed myself. But if it is true that I am you and this is so often how I feel, then I am acting as rightly as I can.

Oh what *am* I saying? To explore this - it seems that I am you here, I am acting not simply on your behalf, but as you would. And this is not a conscious passed-on concept - it is a living felt reality. Similarly yourself, you are not simply yourself, nor are you acting on behalf of Inayat Khan - he does not act as himself (as we think of it) but is an acting vehicle of a greater entity - on forever through to God. Yet through each one, this creative force manifests according to the personality of the vehicle-being, and the times and places. So I am very much myself, and the form of my particular work is brand new right now. You are very much yourself in the same way. In this way the message is always forever new and totally appropriate and absolutely right. Yet it is also forever old and never changing. Only the form changes as humanity evolves through all the changes on earth.

I am writing this to you now so you can see your own voice reflected in my form. Yet never will I reflect to another this particular aspect of being. When I sing in writing to you, you understand who I am. And you must also know by now that my teacher is far beyond me - I have no doubt that in times to come the work will expand terrifically. And when this occurs you must allow Carol to handle the many public aspects. Your age will not defeat you, for at last you are ready to take hold - as has always been promised.

131

I had to stop this writing because it seemed very strange to me. Especially when it came to writing my own name in the 3rd person. I tried to change it to "others" but it simply wasn't possible. Why does this happen to me? Should I let myself go into it, or is it best to not allow it? It happens in my mind as well. When I follow this voice then wonders happen. In the sufi group I depend on it to learn what to do. But I am a little scared of what I've heard about automatic writing. Yet I trust what is said so implicitly. Everytime I sit down to write this happens (unless I keep myself really tight and don't allow it.) Such a fountain, I am continually amazed.

Do you feel this is real or delusion?

Love,

Carol

You know the message isn't finished, and you also know what is right and true. I would never deceive you for I am you. Now you understand. It is simply a way of getting through the logical mind - to establish a dichotomy. But I am here to tell you there is no separation in being - we are all one. Nothing is "other" - all is *me, all* is *you,* for *all* is *one.* This is the only truth - alive one vibrant living being - love it all as yourself - it is you.

Oh Shamcher, what is this all about?

May 5, 1976

Dear Carol,

Your precious letter says "May 1st" so the first letter in your collection, perhaps it should be last. They are all so good but now I think this is the very best.

Should you "let yourself go"? Yes. Should you hold back? No. But you should always watch carefully, like a Gnana Yogi, whose intelligence always flames brightly upon all his doings and decisions and so he knows what to do and what not to do. He does not need to stop dead and think "should I let go?" He may thus miss the greatest opportunities. If he seems to have let go too early or in a wrong sense, he can always repair whatever damage. At least that is me. And you are right: there seems no immediate change (except with such sublime beings as yourself) but the seed has been sown and will grow, so don't worry, don't fret. You have done yours. Nature or God will do the rest. You will never learn the right approach without trying, trying all the time. So don't hold back. Go ahead. So few do. But with care and wisdom of course. Be bold, be daring, and be ready to study the effects and change if you should. But no two people require the same approach, that is where the churches and movements do their bad stuff. They try to put all into the same form. We had a lot of talks about that in California yesterday. A student is writing his thesis on "new religious impulses and their effect on the society - economically, sociologically, internationally." One whole chapter on the sufi effort. He "taped" for three hours.

Yes yes Carol you are acting as I would and often better.

You needn't be scared of what you are doing for it is entirely different from "automatic" writing, besides even that would not defeat you, now (but don't try it, please, for other reasons we may go into.) With your present development, specially your independence, above all psychic nonsense, none of the lower beings could get hold of you or come near you, and the *Ya Rafa Ya Dafa* will further help.

Oh, beautiful, divine Carol, only one in a million can drown in the ocean of *love*.

Shamcher

May 10, 1976

Dear dear Shamcher,

As I write to you tonight my heart is so open. Please always know that this wide open channel exists and that whatever work there is which you feel I should do, I will gladly undertake. How else can I show you my unending gratitude and forever caring?

It feels particularly strong tonight as I sit here writing to you, with the flowering gardenia plant on the table. The baby is moving within me.

One of the ways I can help is to follow my intuition strongly, clearly, and without a hint of hesitation. This is growing as I grow - oh, how can I tell you of how the seed you planted and tended is just bursting in blooms? But this is still so young, such a beginning.

With our first contact I felt myself beginning to flower within - now I wish to send you all of the fragrance of this flowering. Somehow, it is just a perseverance in this sufi work (in myself and outerly with others, the spontaneous sharing) this is part of the way the fragrance spreads.

So I surround you through the air, through the mind and all through your heart, surround you that I may be consumed entirely in your beautiful being. In this way I can barely describe the process of deep love I feel is expressing through us, and through all we meet.

It's late now. I dream your splendid self – whoever you are, whoever I am doesn't matter for this oneness of love is all we can be, the depth and breadth of being.

Love,

Carol

May 17, 1976

Dear Carol,

Enclose two copies of letter from Pir Vilayat showing that now your group is official also from Pir Vilayat's point of view, besides from mine, and also, according to him, you are the leader and also, although according to him only the "Seraj un Munir", the top cherag, Pir Vilayat, can ordain cherags, but he accepts my ordination as valid now, "anticipatory". However in Inayat Khan's organization it was not only the Seraj-un-Munir who could ordain cherags. I was ordained by a sheik, Baron Van Tuyll, and the rule they now have is totally unpractical and I shall see to changing it.

Ah, your enclosed letter about travels. Yes, if you really are gouging in money so you can go to New York, a visit to the Abode would be good of course. You will find transportation at least every week from the sufi Khanka in New York City, and my stupidity has mislaid the address but I have it at home, any time you really want to know. I will be at the Abode July 4 and perhaps a few days before. But this whole trip to NY and back will cost me $447 - just for airfare and in my low intelligence I can somehow not imagine that you, at 28, can afford such a price. And if Evelyn in the last moment decides to go along it will be $900 just for airfare. Yes, there may be a future that his majesty Shamcher travels with a host of superior company and assistants but this is not yet, and I really don't like the idea, seems waste of taxpayers money.

Actually, I have no idea whether I shall go east or not. At present it looks like it and there are reservations. But you are a big girl now. You can go to Abode alone and make a queenly appearance and conquer all. I will be in your heart along with all the others. But watch the money. The price seems ridiculous, even for me.

Yes, yes, Carol, wordlessly...

Shamcher

May 18, 1976

Dear Shamcher,

Your letter last and the article you wrote were so great and so very helpful to me. Just helping me to trust myself. You touched on essential matters that just never seem to be expressed - aspects of sufism which somehow aren't explored - but this cannot be true, it is always explored, just not expressed.

Last night before I went to sleep I was suddenly and so very beautifully with you, and it was so intense - indescribable.

Being pregnant is such a job, now the baby is moving and I seem, again, in a new phase full of deep waves of love that come roaring through overwhelming.

I'm sending this love to you at this time - you know, Shamcher, this crystal we share is forever.

Love,

Carol

May 25, 1976

Dear J__,

Since you mentioned Inayat Khan, I have been rumbling through all my hiding places and bookcases and cardboard boxes to find *The Soul, Whence and Whither*, which contains his complete story of what survives and where and by reading it you may feel or sense that he does not repeat tales but speaks of what he sees and knows.

I have had dozens of these books and given them away but none are left. I have ordered a new one and will be sending you shortly.

Meanwhile, against my better judgment, I send you another of his books where only the very last chapter touches upon life and "death", how to think in order to see for yourself. The beginning chapters of this book may also please you for they refer to the lucky ones who see their life's purpose, which you did even at age twenty or thereabout, long before I did, with my life (before in respect to our respective ages, not before in absolute time.) Since you are one of those lucky ones, you will quickly grasp also the matter of survival.

My old friend Koot Hoomi, a splendid yogi from Shigatse, says, "Man thinks of himself as solid. He lives within an envelope of flesh and blood that is penetrated by his consciousness. Consciousness must be regarded as man's connection with his source, and its flexibility as man's greatest asset; yet, when wrongly used, it is his greatest weakness. The consciousness of humanity today is so easily influenced by banal and barbaric doings that the magnificent cosmic purpose Heaven has prepared in the creation of man is seldom recognized even minutely. . . In heaven's name, from whence cometh energy? What is it that beats your heart? A wish obviously not your own, or it would not so suddenly terminate. Instead the will of God, the desire of God, beats your heart. Men's lives would not be paltry then, if they also let Him determine their consciousness and their thoughts. . . "

Best regards,

Bryn

May 25, 1976

Oh, lovely Carol, if your letters, your golden jewelled letters wouldn't come regularly I don't know how I could hold out, in spite of the fact that we always are together, no, always one. Yet, your letters feed me, thrill me, make me a new person every time, because I am physical beside spiritual, mental, emotional and etheric.

There is still one letter from you I have lost temporarily, but I will find it again.

About all these rules and regulations the order have and you are a bit worried about - remember that Pir Vilayat, obedient to his father and always overworked listens to those close to him, some of which are as good as they could be, others not, and they change back and forth and the whole cabale is not worth a nickel but you learn to smile and laugh and take it all quietly without breaking into a rage - except occasionally when it is required. Here the other year when you had sixth degree you could initiate others so I rapidly initiated some into that degree. Then at the next meet I was told the degree at which you could initiate was seven. So I smiled and said, "So seven it will be now despite your decision a year ago" and had to initiate all these people, wherever I could find them, anew. But the sly fellow who had initiated the change perhaps just wanted to thwart my independent actions. But Pir Vilayat knows that if he is not careful, ignoring the sly and pay attention to me and my friends, he would lose us quick and he would not like that at all. He does not remember what he said, before, and then changes back again but sometimes confusion rules. But this is the same in every spiritual or nonspiritual organization. It does not really matter at all. Whatever officials say, continue quietly to do the essentials and if necessary simply ignore their remonstrations. There are some rules that I have completely circumscribed.

Pir Vilayat has to go through the same bitter experiences his father went through. None of them knew the traps of organization as well as I do. Carol you are wonderful and I love you.
Shamcher

June 2, 1976

Carol, you lovely genius,

I could laugh and giggle about your beautiful attached letter which I had lost and found again. You are right, these matters are not now explored except through a few minds such as yours and mine. Isn't it incredible? We have to deliver a message to poor little *man* (including woman - man means both here, all.)

Most people, including most sufis and yogis are running for teachers today, and in a sense that is good, but in this running they forget their glorious selves, in whom they should have more and deeper faith and confidence. Like most scientists, who take statistics from superficial observations and from such seedy inexactness make laws or theories - without ever seeking into his own soul where deeper truths are hidden and against which all his light-weight statistics should be weighed and evaluated. A "teacher" is simply an anomaly.

Oh, Carol, you will have an enormous task when I go to the eternal hunting ground. But of course you have nothing whatever to fear, whatever happens. You have God himself behind you, what more could there be? As Hidayat said: His father, Inayat Khan, was not perfect, handled the organization as many older sufis had, but then gradually he woke up to greater truths. So with all the teachers. We can respect them all but not deify them, for they were all wrong, although of good intentions. No, let me change that; they may have seen all that we need now but understood that the world was not ready at the time. No again: They may have tried, they may have said things that were buried and forgotten until we dug it up. We must try to lead this way through the sufis, not against them, for they deserve the truth.
Love,
Shamcher

June 2, 1976

My dear Hidayat,

It was so delightful to hear you and talk with you. You have added a most precious aspect of your father's message and will, to the combined sufi effort. I feel so good about this particularly because I have felt at the last meeting with your father before he went to India exactly those aspects that you are now representing.

Also, I realize that many people, perhaps most people, may be reached and involved through the kind of organization your father had at first, in tune with so many older sufi orders. I have gone even further: watching Sam Lewis, a disciple of your father, gather a flock around him, I suggested to Pir Vilayat he should make their acquaintance and achieve a cooperation. And eventually he did, and in a different and possibly more efficient manner than I had envisaged. So I am deeply involved in this game and his entire mission as I am in yours. From an outward standpoint, both contribute to the total message and to the strategy of presenting and involving.

Hidayat and Pir Vilayat, each exclusively and both jointly, live in and fill joyfully my heart.

Love,

Shamcher

June 7, 1976

Dear Beloved Carol,

Thank you for your beautiful letter from Edmonton to Cleveland. After a rousing week there, came the Abode, at New Lebanon New York, wild lonely country and many hundred-year-old huge wooden houses and barns and a campsite for 60 people high above all that. (There were 400 at the camp before.)

I heard with a bit of alarm about your illness. I trust you have arranged things in a lighter vein and that you are marching strongly and ably toward the great event.

After the Abode we went to Unadilla, another even more beautiful sufi community; a large beautiful common house, and then other small houses that the mureeds have built spread over the 100 acres they possess and out of sight of each other. The most beautiful hilly country, 3-4 hours drive from the big city of New York where we are now, having the three top floors in 242 East 14th Street. On the street below you can buy and experience absolutely

138

everything. It means so much to New York to have this oasis of joyful power in its midst.

When asked to conduct a meditation and a class at the Abode, I called upon all the others to lead - two minutes each. Only when there was no one willing did I inflict upon them a little story from Inayat's life. That fired them again.

Love,
Shamcher

July 7, 1976

Dearest Shamcher,

It's been a strange time, without any letters from you. All is well - beauty upon beauty, difficulty upon difficulty - all flowing daily. How I miss your letters!

I could tell you some of what is happening here, but I feel like all I want is to be close to you. Nothing means anything to me but that beautiful sharing of the river of spirit. I yearn for this only. I feel it could somehow be totally within myself - why must I connect with this through other people to be awakened in myself? Yet, it seems stronger to me in the connection.

Now this connection is sometimes with Inayat Khan, who can't be called "another person" - and often it's far across the miles, or spheres, or worlds, but still there is always another, there is a relationship. I know in my heart that this is a limited view, and that soon this "relationship" will blast apart, revealing itself to be totally made up as a vehicle for growth into true understanding, being.

But here I falter, because I don't live what I'm writing about - I'm still in the stage of needing another who guides, who resonates, responds, etc. I feel a premonition that this soon will fall away.

My love and gratitude flow to you forever,
Carol

July 14, 1976

Dear Carol and company,

Home to lovely letter from *you*. Home without voice, for the muggy heat of New York sent me flopping up to Martha's Vineyard, the paradise island in Massachusetts. The ocean was bitterly cold and I thought, as of yore, Dive in, you coward. And not only did I dive in against all my better feelings, but stayed in and swam far out; after days of this, I developed a painful cough which gradually I am ridding myself of.

And on the plane, just before landing in Seattle I threw off my seat belt and bounced for the bathroom where four husky stewardesses tried their best to stop me, and pounded on the wall continually and when I finally emerged they carried me off to a nearby seat (not my real seat) and plunked me down and put the belt around me as if it was the electric chair. This was the first time no stewardess smiled at me when we left.

More later,

Love,

Shamcher

July 12, 1976

Dear Shamcher

So often my heart has swelled up and opened wide to you. I wonder now at my audacity and arrogance ever to have thought that we are the same, that I am equal to you and that somehow I am a continuation of your fine dynamic fire. Beside you I am a little child and when you play with me I feel to be on your level - through this play I learn and grow. My feeling for you is not child-like, but as developed as possible for me. When I become overwhelmed by your great beauty and strength I am perhaps too burned up to love you with any art or finesse - it just gets blind. So you take care not to shine too brilliantly - it seems you shine to me as much as I can handle.

I am so eternally grateful to you for the blessing of our contact, so much could be said - but where are the words? You know, far better than I do, just what this is. Or do you know? Are you like me and just open? Oh more so - for it is you who first opened my heart. You know, the second letter you sent me (ever in our time this time) took me off into another world. I saw and felt a being who formally embraced me and kissed both cheeks. Later I recognized this was Inayat Khan (from a photo I saw it was him!)

I have missed your letters, but your presence within me beautifully is like a long chain that goes deep within - from being to being.

A young man who lived at the Abode for a time has turned up here, of all places, and it's encouraging to be with him. Because he knows dances, we will probably begin doing them. Though I always emphasize that this is just icing on the cake, that the real depth of sufism is fathomed by the way of the heart. Oh how painful this way is and how beautiful the opening! It is a continuous birthing of the spirit - over and over again. Unending opening.

I need more help at this time for there is a birthing going on in me - as this child within me grows to birth, I feel a change in my spirit (whose spirit?) and when this baby is born, I'll be born too. Oh Shamcher, so tenderly, with tears and deep love I send you this deep and subtle feeling.

Be well.

Forever in love,

Carol

P.S. Hugs and kisses in all the spheres - all beings sing and dance!

July 14, 1976

Dear Shamcher,

I've just finished writing to people about various organizational things and in a way I'm troubled. Part of the trouble is that I see how very much I'm tuned to the organizational world. A form of inspiration flows through organization as a medium for the manifestation of the spirit. But part of me holds back - I don't like organization, nor do I wish to devote my time to it for I get swallowed in it and the alone time I so need just goes. Yet I recognize a gift in it, and will not deny that aspect of my being. It is just strange and frightening to me. Because I can organize stuff and make decisions and catalyze all sorts of action, yet here is still me just working on myself with so very far to go to get to a place to begin the inner work. I'm afraid that my facility in the outer work will cause me to let go or slough over the inner. I can, however, see it all as one.

Many worlds are opening to me and I am amazed. But I've been feeling more and more ordinary and just a regular pregnant lady all the time. I've been buried in my body, the focus has narrowed right down to me in this body with this baby inside. And *my* emotions, *my* everything. Then to sit and write these letters just crashes open a vast vista.

Are you better from your sore throat now? Have you received the lozenges of love I sent you by air?

Please write me whenever you can.

Love,

Carol

P.S. We are moving to the country this fall.

141

July 19, 1976

Dearest Shamcher,

It was good to get your letter and know that you are now home safe and sound. I trust that your throat is better by now and that all is well.

I feel as you do that this is best: to let the hierarchy go into a more free-flowing system - here at any instant anyone will be bearing the strength of the message clearly, then at any time it shifts to another as the life force flows through the appropriate channels for the manifestation of the work. The way things are now is based on inner guidance and clear contact with Inayat Khan and all others, yet this is filtered through one's belief system. So everyone is right, and no doubt fulfilling purpose - there is no need to negate another view but simply to expand your own to include it. Why can't all these ways be tolerated by the sufis - or must everyone lockstep to the same tune?

The damage done by the "one-way" attitude is that seekers feel they must adapt themselves to some already-existent system, rather than cultivate their own gardens to see what the blooms will be! Not all of us are growing snap dragons, or roses for that matter - some are peonies and some are mixed vegetables, and each is a gift at a particular time. Not necessarily *all the time* is the peony considered the perfect bloom. (And how ridiculous for carrots, roses and dandelions to masquerade as peonies!)

And yet, organization seems to include some sort of established system and framework in which to grow. I see the framework as a net, constantly flexing. It would be best to look at the present need of the times - to see where the present way functions beneficially and where there are holes and needs unfulfilled in this way. It seems like this to me: Since Inayat Khan's passing we are all acting as his body - carrying on the work in a deeper and more multi-octaved form than the form of one human being could ever be - no matter how vast. As this flow of inspiration through us causes us to act in the way we feel is appropriate, we all carry out the work. Now it seems that the feet get one message and the toes another - which is greater, the foot or the toe? That hardly matters when the issue is whether the whole foot is going in one unified direction.

Really, the only people who understand the hierarchy-less approach feel it in their being - the independence and total trust within and without. This happens through hierarchies and not through hierarchies, though through sometimes takes longer.

Enough of this ranting. I'll end this letter - with still so much to say to

you dearest shining beam.
Love forever,
Carol

July 31, 1976

Dear Carol,

How explicitly you describe your two pulls organization-wise. You know, if you decide to have nothing more to do with organizations that would be fine with me and I hope with you. Or you could decide to let someone else do all the organizational work, equally fine.

I live violently outside all organization, making people crazy, not knowing what to do with me. Actually, though, you are not neglecting the inner by organizing - on the contrary, you are learning inner through outer. In a sense this is how I work organizations: Make them inner. As on the Western Front with those Belgians - the most excellent organization is not being organized from the outside but letting it inner-organize itself. This is what I hope some day to do with the whole Sufi Order.

I am tired now. Can't eat, have no appetite, seem to want very much to go to the other hunting grounds - oh yes, thank you, your good heart lozenges reached me and did good, but there is an empty feel about my midriff as if life is leaving....

Your whole outfit there is my great good heir and rock, so never worry.
Love,
Shamcher

August 5, 1976

Dearest Shamcher,

Your last letter stirred so many feelings in me. I knew you were feeling unwell and I'm certainly sending what I can to you as comfort, strength and get-well loves. Yet a part of me says that this is not what you need right now - what is it that you need and how can I possibly help?

I trust that always we are together and my love in you will grow forever. No one is as true in thought and action as you are and have been - you have taught me such trust and giving.

Perhaps by the time you receive this letter you will be eating more and feeling more in this world and less in the next. I sincerely hope so and trust

143

that you will not yet go. My feeling here is accepting of whatever comes - I could thrash around wildly, begging you to hang on, to finish your work, to wait until you meet this baby I'm having, and all the reasons I can't know and more - but I won't. You know my feelings here. All I can do, as you, is simply accept and send you love, love, love as an encircling blanket.

Love,

Carol

P.S. There is no way I would let all organization go, but I must learn to give the work to others, to spread it around.

August 8, 1976

Dearest Shamcher,

Let this letter be a light to your already brilliant being! I've been just now overwhelmed by a wave of feeling which is directed toward you in the most beautiful forms of all affections and love. Let it all cascade through, cleansing and healing you in beauty and love.

So I sat down to write to you - this moment you receive all these feelings and the letter you read days later is just a token of the energies. However you are feeling at this time, I feel linked with you in a symbiotic contact, where I provide what you need sometimes and you provide what I need others. Yet this is just how it appears; more deeply. . . I won't go further in metaphysical nattering on. Let me caress you in warm love and bathe you forever in light.

How can I further open to your beautiful being than to offer you all love, all my self and acting being? You showed me trueness in my own heart, now I offer this to you - forever.

Love,

Carol

August 12, 1976

Dear Carol,

Don't I have a lovely lazy time writing letters? Just sending the beautiful perfect letters I receive from the world's expert letter-writer as if they were my own? When does this book come out? I can't wait much longer. Also you sent me so many loving thoughts or rather feelings that now I am coming back from the dead and am among the living again.

Blessed love,

Shamcher

August 17, 1976

Dear Shamcher,

So so good to hear from you and to know that you are feeling better. Gary is working on fixing up the house we'll soon be living in, and I am more pregnant every day. How wonderful to be in this blessed state, with a new little person growing inside.

I see all of humanity as a river-sea, a long chain of beings, one inside the other. And temporarily, in this body, I am aware of being both a separate person and beyond it completely. Such feelings bring me to thoroughly enjoy the present and look forward with a great push to the future life!!!

Friends are so kind in these days, as I wait in the last month for the baby to appear. It could be a chance for the people who take part in the sufi group to become more active and self-sufficient - I'll be in baby world but they will continue. Yet I wonder if there is anybody who is so committed to this work that he/she would take on the bulk of this work - organizing, etc. I know I must certainly continue until some one or two or more do. Maybe this time of me being "out of the picture" will bring new energies to the fore. I can't ask for anything or anyone - unless it feels totally right. Those closest are least into organizing! But I can't just let it go, the energy has to grow, maybe we need new forms.

I love you and trust you as friend, teacher and self.

Please write - I send you all love.

Carol

P.S. Thank you for getting better and being well.

P.S. Again. I'm looking like the Venus of Willendorf - enormously pregnant - a ripe pod.

P.S. I closed up the letter but found there was more to say. It seems to me that I must use this organizational gift in a very subtle way, so that the physical stuff happens on its own and inner work is more to the fore. The inner focus must never be lost.

To begin in this way is difficult, as there aren't immediate physical results, but this is bound to come. It's foolish and impossible to work from the physical out to the more spiritual - they must be linked as *one* or else the focus should be spirit rather than matter. It seems so strange to me to lead people in singing, for example, and know that the attachment to such a practice is of no help whatsoever. And furthermore it seems in some way to hinder. People are so ready to take it on and paste it on any outer form - yet

145

within there must be a cataclysmic inner shaking of all seeming foundations - over and over again.

Then, of course, comes the other extreme of the "teacher" who breaks through such stuff - causing an equal dependence upon himself/herself acting as catalyst - I've met people addicted to big cheeses and zonds and energy transfers which cause shattering, but then. . . where is the inner self-reliance and awakening of the inner directive force? As I see all this (with my little limited view) I wonder where it leads and how it is possible for people to get through their own blocks and preconceptions. The only answer is to trust and love God in your heart and in all. This will lead truly to the source.

So often I see someone who is awake - so beautiful - yet asleep to that beauty and to that vitality of being which is so obvious to me - it is as a beacon. I dive in love with them before I know what's happening. Sometimes it is so beautiful, sometimes I touch my own (or whose?) fears of going further. In that place what is mine? I can't tell. Why do I write all this to you? Part of the way I love you, I guess, is to show you this as it flows through.

This is a long PS and I'll end with deepest affection and eternal gratitude.

Love love love,

Carol

August 26, 1976

Dear Carol,

You are so perfectly right about starting the organization - starting everything - from within and not from without, but more than that: you are so perfectly right at seeing straight at things and not living a life of futile expectations. Many want to see, not the present facts, but some promise of the future, such as: If they stay with me and do exercises with me they would be powerful, able to command their friends, know their thoughts and outwit them. So, should one let them come and be bitterly disappointed when they find out there is no ambition here, nor any chance of overpowering and outwitting your brothers and sisters? Or let them keep the distance so they never find out?

There is a temptation to speak in nationalities: American and Canadian, but that is not really fair. There are some Canadians and some Americans of both types; the type who sees and understands, the type who anticipates and doesn't understand.

So what does one do? I do both: Call them here to find out, let them stay here and not find out - at least not here. But am I right? Of course not. Who is right? Or wrong? We act. That is all. And learn. And become very humble, seeing how wrong we were, and yet, were we wrong? Of course not. We did our thing, the way we saw it at the time. Again, as you say, if the inner is allowed to govern. . . .

Carol, where do you go next? Why Carol, excuse me, but you are already next. You are already there. What is time? A weird earthly delusion. What is next? It is now or earlier. And yet, when all these people come to you and say "Where do we go next?" you have to have an answer, you cannot always say to them: you are already there, for that may confuse them. So you hear what the planner wants to do next and you let him - they - try it. But for me, all the way down here, that would be high-handed, to imagine I could tell you, except of course if you want me to. But actually you don't want me to. You want to go your own way, and you should, and let the decision flow smoothly from your combined spirits, inner.

Love, dear Carol

dear, dear,

Shamcher

September 1, 1976

Dear Shamcher,

As you see, I have a typewriter again, and have been working on the book. What an experience it has been typing these: I seem to go right into that time (whatever time it was) and come back to "normal" life after typing in a daze, half here, half there. I'd like to get it done before the baby comes as I'll be so busy then, adjusting to a new little one.

In the world of organization, I am leaving it for the moment and letting things take their course. I'll concentrate on the baby and my own life within. When things in the family are settled I will put effort into encouraging people to do more. In future I will be shining out more, rather than in, for the sun shines in to the baby right now as my time draws very near.

Our house in the country is almost finished and I'm so grateful to the friends who have come out on weekends to help with the work of painting and fixing it up. It will be such a fine place to live, filled as it is with the loving help of so many good friends. I am just so grateful.

How is your health now?

What I said in the last letter I repeat in this one, though why I really don't know; and that is, where do I go from here? Yes you answered me beautifully and it is so. Yet I feel that there is a clue from you which will be helpful to me in the directions to go. When I ask within, the answer comes to ask you, so here I am, in this place of not knowing or really caring (as it will unfold to me in time) but asking anyways. I know it must be right to ask you to help me in this as I feel my heart opening wide when I write to you now. As you said, I do so want my own way, really I can do nothing else, so this questioning is remarkable - except that I have always related to you as to my inner self, and so you are. In words this seems badly expressed but you understand, I trust.

Love, forever and always,

Carol

September 3, 1976

Dear Carol,

Your beautifully typed letter makes me so humble and ashamed and also thinking of how much time and effort you must have spent while so many other things are pressing you. I am simply delighted to hear that you are typing the book already, maybe to adequately feed and house the coming species.

Now I am a bit concerned about what you said about your friend, that she was so shocked and surprised (and perhaps vomiting?) because of my letter. I had not the fortunate chance of writing her, as I did you, before I had met her but only after. I thought I knew her and now she is shocked and turned away. Actually, you know, when I receive a letter I let it rest until words and sentences in response come surging through my head and I don't know where those words come from but I promptly write them down and send them. Now it may be that those are the words this person needs whether she or he thinks so or not, but then again they may come from a special devil temporarily occupying my pink hair and maybe, I have often thought, you should and I should be careful not personally to see these tender souls in Edmonton who are really your business, not mine. So please tell me as frankly and as brutally as possible about her reaction and what will happen now. And also tell me your own personal reaction to that letter, that upset her so.

Now your question: Where do I go next? Oh, Carol, don't you remember that I never prophesy? That is robbing God of his options. The

148

worst possible blunder. I see a million wonderful prospects for you and to mention even one of them would blaspheme God. Still, that is what all the "psychics" do, all the time, and how much better if these psychics spent all their time chopping wood. Nonono Carol, I have no idea even about my own tomorrow, far less of yours. But that it is great, wonderful, challenging, that is all we may say. So yesyesyes you are right in asking, for it is the cry of the soul, wanting to go where it should, and you are equally right in not expecting a reply in so many words except as above stated.

And tell me please, when or what did I tell you that you saw as Inayat Khan healing practices and so told your friend? I am not in the healing business which to me is a slight interference in God's plans, but automatically my breath goes out to every living thing and, I hope, may do what some call heal, but not to my humble knowledge. Sitara said I was the only one who completely raised her from the dead - when she was dead from a heart attack five years ago. But actually it was herself. My own health? Thank you, seems on top, excellent just now, never was better.

Love, the only thing that lasts and lasts,
Shamcher

September 12, 1976

Dear Carol,

How marvelous - you keep up a beautiful correspondence in impeccable typing while just about to have a baby and at the same time moving to your country estate. . . yes, do you know that I have in fact often thought about how happy it would be to live in your Canadian country community. So I was very happy about your invitation, but is it not as Pir Vilayat said about another invitation: Something I would so much like to do but will probably never do? For even if I may be welcome by you - what about all the others? - and then there is Evelyn, would she want to?

Speaking of moving: I thought I never could again, especially seeing how Evelyn has bought and stored in the most strange places - it seemed unsolvable. Then I started, while Evelyn was in the hospital, realized I couldn't do everything but enjoyed more and more what I could do and ended up with 26 cartons plus a mattress and two chairs - all the other furniture I simply left, it was worn and torn, and to a nervous former landlord I said, Use it or throw it away, charge me for any expenses - and then the movers came, at 8:30 morning and 9:30 we were all moved into the new apartment,

149

a cosy little second storey with bath on the first floor, all electric, cheaper than the other, much nicer and more comfortable, huge yard, unfortunately no garage. It was Evelyn's choice. Yes, so now I have learned the art of moving. I complimented the fast movers and they in turn complimented me, on readiness and no fuss.

All my love,

Shamcher

September 15, 1976

Dear Shamcher,

We are still waiting for the baby and still waiting for the house to be ready. I am becoming stronger every day as I feel this baby coming. It is so amazing that I am being born with this child just as I died with Cory.

Life is suddenly very rich for me. There is so much in and out to do and to experience and to express and to enjoy. The world seems to be full of just everything imaginable all manifesting at the same time all the varieties of possibilities that could ever be. Yet all I want is to feel it simpler, and for it to be calmer, more simplicity and openness than before, where people can openly love one another and share those tender exchanges which are all we can really give one another - ourselves, continuously each day over and over again.

I must go now, be well, take care, and remember how I love you, dream you, care for you in all ways, always and in every way.

Tenderly,

Carol

September 29, 1976

My dearest Shamcher,

Our baby came - a girl! Her name is Christina Rose and we call her Rosie. She certainly is rosy and she really is so incredibly beautiful. She's one week old today - and there are no words at all to express our deep love for her. And how it has changed me! Just exactly what I need to learn all about loving and tending and protecting and caring, so strongly, all over again.

I wanted to tell you all about her but really nothing can be said - she seems miraculous to me and though her body formed inside mine, she comes from far beyond. And we have the joy and responsibility of teaching her earthly ways.

My life is very simple now - a little cocoon of Rosie and her needs. Gary is so loving and supportive. We have been brought even closer by this little girl. Though my life is simple, physically it is chaos - we've been moving to the country and our house isn't finished - all quite stressful but somehow we muddle through. There has been so much help from friends.
Love,
Carol

October 5, 1976

Dear Carol,

Whatever it is, it is beautiful, it is right, because it is you. I have been thinking a lot about you these days, assume you are flat on your back and cannot write, while doing your tremendous, holy and sacred thing. I am with you. What more can I say just now?
Love,
Shamcher

October 8, 1976

Carol!

A baby girl - what a wonder. For it seems that increasingly the women are taking over. But remember: I can make no predictions, robbing God of his options so I don't even know if Rosie will go along with what we are doing or be entirely different, for example a great plant scientist who knows everything about plants. You don't predict the lives entrusted to us. They are not entrusted to us for the purpose of predicting but so we can give them all the freedom and means to follow what is in their souls. What a wonderful thing you have channeled.

I hope the letters I lately sent to 12730 102 Avenue will be forwarded, specially since there were some tremendous letters from you enclosed in the envelopes.

Do I enclose a letter to that friend of yours? Tell me if the letter is right or wrong, and I don't tell her I sent it to you. I don't feel entitled to send you hers.

Oh, so much more to say, about my feelings for you and Rosie and Gary and you-all.
Love,
Shamcher

151

October 27, 1976

Dearest: Shamcher,

At last there is some time to write you. Caring for Rosie, plus the household tasks are about all I ever have time for these days, though somehow I manage also to keep on with the radio program and from time to time teach some classes. It is amazing how time goes - for me it seems to be marked from feeding time to feeding time. It is most beautiful to have this child Rosie, though sometimes I find that I need a little more sleep than I get.

All this time of coming back to myself after the birth, you have been clearly and so beautifully on my mind and shining in my heart, as a light and a guide and a love. I feel so much greater a dedication to the path of truth than ever before and at the same time a much finer appreciation of everyday life - the moments are so precious. It seems that now I can more clearly feel the struggle within myself between that aspect which closes me down from the beauty, closing me from following my intuition and the self, whatever glimmerings there may be. As my own struggle is coming clearer, and it seems that there is so much work ahead, there is the whole side of my being which other people seem to see, a side which I don't even know. How strange that when I'm feeling not particularly "spiritual", in fact totally exhausted with the life of a new mother, that someone should say that my presence would lift him out of himself. More and more this seems to be happening around me.

This plus a rumor, which came back to me from a series of friends, that I am a self-styled guru who hypnotizes people in order to boost my own ego. It makes me feel very strange and so very confused. It's so ludicrous, really, and totally untrue, but at the same time the rumor caused me to do some soul-searching to see just what I am doing, and why and how. The answer which came is that I am acting as I must in every situation and whatever others perceive is their own business.

I feel that soon I will return to encouraging more sufi activity here again. I let things lapse and just focused on the birth, moving and everyday living. But somehow I am drawn, and I should get things together and begin weekly meetings again. It made me feel sad, or at least, look again at what I had done, the way of working, that caused it to go the way it did, for when I let the meetings go, there was no one who as yet felt strongly enough to carry them on. But that takes time, I suppose, and a specific feeling. I suppose I'm living too much in the future. In a little while I'll try again.

It would be beautiful to spend some time with you again. We have so much to share, and the time is passing very quickly. It seems vital. Not just because I would love to see you and be with you or because this place would benefit so from your presence, but also because I feel ready for some sort of change and to be with you will no doubt catalyze. Now in some ways saying these things could be setting up expectations, but with you, dearest Shamcher, all has always been right and perfect and as it should be in time and space. However it will be, really we must be together again, not just for me, but for you as well, for together we share a beautiful magic. As the love pours through me to you, it feels calm and clear and without a single agitated ripple - steady, always clear.

Love,

Carol

November 3, 1976

Dear Dear Carol,

What vibrating words. You know your rumor that you hypnotize people to boost your ego as a great guru - that always happens to people on the path and to me it rumbles my insides in a colossal belly-laugh, and for several reasons: First it is so funny and so typical of some people's thinking - people who will be there some day, who approach it in what may seem an uncouth way now but nevertheless it is an approach. And for you? Gooder than good. For it keeps you on your toes. If there is ever a doubt, a feeling of unpleasantness about it, watch out, there may be still a little weed, and root it out! But if there is only benevolent belly-laugh - be glad. Embrace the wonderful rumor-monger. Who is it? Do you know? You should call him/her your guru for the time being. But not for long.

Did Rosie get a note? A dirty USA note? For her birthday?

I see you have received the famous "Messenger" with only figures. I am sorry. I have heard tell about it, not yet received it.

About coming: Yes, I think some time, but no travel expenses payment accepted, not yet anyhow. I may be so poor one day I'll need it, but then, who knows, I may not travel. Yes, I really feel a visit would be good, and for you-all there would be no money expense, but you might have to take care of me while I am there.

As to what you should do or not do in the way of organization, well, wonderful Carol, who am I to say? That is entirely up to you, and not only

153

to you but to you every moment of your life. So that you need not make any decision today of what you will do tomorrow. Indeed, how could you? Or I? You are guided by your superior, to your view perhaps whimsical, wonderful. highest, God-nearest self and who would be fool enough to interfere with *that*?

Oh Carol, it was so good to hear from you again and you are so right, so right, in every word that ensues from your pages.

Love to all of you,

Shamcher

November 4, 1976

Dear Carol,

How is your book of letters coming? What did the publishers you have submitted it to say so far?

Here is another riddle. She is 18, shooting up like a splendid plant, throwing teachers around in a whirl, skimming their cream, or thinking she does. Now she has entrusted me with her address, told me to write if I care, thinking I will add to the melee, giving hints, practices, your know-all. For weeks and weeks her address has burned in my pocket. I cannot find a thing to write her. I should perhaps write and tell her she is so perfect she needs no more teaching, or just that she needs no more teaching, especially from me, since I am no teacher at all. Then she can continue and go and learn from other non-teachers (who do not know they are non-teachers, so they teach her, or think they do.) You know, you have a responsibility for me and my letters and my behavior now, so you better tell me promptly what to do. She reminds me of that woman in Woodstock who screamed at me for building torpedoes. But now this woman is as deeply devoted to me as anyone. Kisses me on the snout and weeps whenever we meet. Writes enthused letters. Says I have solved the mystery between her and her husband, even though I didn't even know she was married.

I am going to write the 18 year old that she is so great, so precious, that poor little me does not know what she needs, so l am consulting my great guide and teacher.

Love for you and Rosie and All your beautifuls,

Shamcher

October 31, 1976

Dear D___,

You seem well on your way, two hours ahead of me, more if we count the time change. Now all that matters is the attitude. Could you possibly see clearly that this leads you to whatever you wish and that the only temporary delay may be caused by you, not the outside world, but whatever is caused by you will certainly disappear very soon (no time determination please! "Soon" is not measured in hours but in effort or visions.) And if you temporarily prefer to be watched by your thoughts rather than the other way around, okay for the time being. No fuzz no cuss. Pray, you say, by the way whom do you pray to? If your meditation is following a certain thought sequence, a certain pattern, that is certainly work, the hardest. And if it is just trying to listen, that is even harder work. But it may be done better when you stop trying.

Breath, yes. No objection to your breathing occasionally through only one nostril. That is natural, in that going to sleep you usually breathe only through your left, waking up - through your right. If one nostril seems so tight you cannot breathe through it, remember who you are, won't you? You are the commander, not your nostrils. But it sometimes takes a little patience to tell your nostril that. Gradually breathe as you command, even if it requires a little effort and artifice in the beginning. Balance is something you don't know in advance. You may have sufficient idea about it to work toward it. In general: Don't expect to know in advance every detail of what you are working toward. If you did, you didn't need to work toward it.

Politically I am more active than ever and more than in any other field. I keep up a never-ending correspondence. Our most horrendous blunder nowadays is unemployment. Not only is this a curse to everybody seeking a job and everybody who has one and is afraid to speak his mind lest he be fired (into unemployment) but unemployment is also the cause of inflation. Also we have available energy sources that would make oil, coal, nucleonics superfluous. I brought one such source to this country from France in the forties: the Ocean Thermal Difference Energy System. Free. Unpolluting. In the seventies the national Science Foundation finally caught up, now it is boosted by industry and universities...

I feel my sufi work has helped me see what I am convinced is the truth about these things, and given me strength to pursue it. To "keep out of politics" is not my view of what a sufi should do. Politics is the application of sufism to earthlife. Without it we have got nothing. To refuse to act politically

155

is to starve your children, destroy civilization.

Government as such is not a plot, but any organization possesses possibilities of being ugly plots...private businesses, cartels, federal, state and county governments, civil service. The point is turning these organizations to beneficial servants rather than monsters.

Love,

Shamcher

(Shamcher to L___: Much of our work now are symbols, archetypes for later generations to carry out in physical splendour, like the lean travels of a Krishna, Buddha or Christ developed into the lush gardens and ashrams and mosques and churches of the Christians, Hebrews, Hindus and Buddhists.)

November 12, 1976

Dear A__,

Your changes which you write about reminds me of Inayat Khan, "My mind changes all the time, My heart never changes." Just like you - and little me.

What you give me in your letters are never burdens. When you air your feelings and thoughts you inspire and enliven me. I feel them, too, and become richer.

You are so right that talking and answering detailed questions about any physical complaint exhausts one and does not help the complaint, on the contrary. Every physical discomfort is a "disease," lack of ease, that is all, and it is eased, brought back to health, not by detailed discussions or particular medicines but by restoring ease by such means as breathing, contemplation of the unfathomable God (which is us, in essence) and good works in general.

It is so comforting, so reassuring, to have your beautiful letter. So many write to me, "Shamcher, I am trying to learn and live God's will for me, and I am just falling all the time, understanding less, sinning more" and at their doorstep they have the remedies, the practices, the means of gradual achievement. But it must be instant, without any effort, without any practice. ... and so it goes.

Lovingly,

Shamcher

November 25, 1976

Dearest Shamcher,

I'm writing now in a strange state - half here, half there, but where here and there are I couldn't ever tell you. So much has been happening in the past few days, I cannot begin to describe. . but now I sit writing to you, feeling on the brink of an immediacy which will no longer wait.

It is as if the rug had been pulled out from under me, leaving everything topsy-turvy.

The other night with my friend was an indescribable teaching for me, and I'd like to share it with you but I know that words are useless here. And I did share it with you, and all, and here again vocabulary limits. I was in very deep waters and somehow acted totally, rightly, through such direct guidance that there was no relationship with this guiding force, *I was It*. And it was all for her in some beautiful dance she shone for the first time in this place far beyond herself. What can I say? There is an inkling now in me of how very vast this journey is, how absolutely beyond the wildest concept I could possibly entertain. You are me and I am you and we are nothing at all, and everything.

None of it takes place on earth (as we know it) at all. We transform the world through our love. We love through our "death" and in this is the continual renewal of all life. Life is everlastingly fed through this miraculous death/life/love which enables us to act. I am sure that action (not as we know it) can only take place from beyond action. It is a pouring of pure love/life/force/essential creativity. My faith - oh what a little word - my commitment is so strengthened. So many fears have stepped out of the way. Still I feel there is a cord keeping me back - but I so trust this miraculous beauty who burns and renews in a glance.

Love,

Carol

December 6, 1976

Dear Carol,

You are becomingly modest about "the difference." The difference between you and almost everybody else is that they flaunt some "teaching" they have parroted. You never do. What you say or write is from your own heart and from the deep layers of your own heart. Genuine. Oh, when I see all the parroting going on, I wonder if there ever was a single teacher. God save me from being a teacher. As for me, I am only me. As for the penetrating spirit, we are all that and when we realize it we write like you, not like Mr. and Ms. Parrot. But the name is a misnomer for a real parrot knows he is a parrot and laughs of himself. But the human parrot thinks he is somebody.

So I send your new masterpiece back - and - when is the glorious book coming out? In the press yet?

Love,
Shamcher

December 14, 1976

Dear Carol,

Just sending you some news. Met a young red-haired-and-bearded actor who just came from you and is going back. Wanted to know if you are holding meetings. I said, yes, in any real sense. He asked if he could bring back a message to you. I said, after much and deep contemplation: Yes, say "HI" from me. So that is from me through him to you.

I am dissolved in you, Carol, and it is so delightful. I no longer exist, you alone exist. Or do you?

Love,
Shamcher

Dear K__,

And this, in a sense, is just an excuse to write you a continuation to my reply to your interesting question how I conciliate Murshid's writing with my view on hierarchies (a view changing gently like a wheat field in a soft breeze.) When you come to the qutubs and walis we are in a field where I have no judgment. My judgment is only in the field where I have or share a responsibility. The field where grades and titles are dispensed by us. In that latter field it is my impression that Inayat Khan changed his mind, as we all do, throughout his years with us, based on his experience and reading our minds, and future minds.

As to qutubs and walis I sometimes wonder whether I am in that line, somewhere, since detailed dispositions of the goodies of the world, energy, economy, international relations are so agonizingly on my mind that they mean more than my little personal life. My wild travels all over the world, covering all continents with as yet no convictions, my later advisory missions, my present heroic fight against PhDs, Nobel Laureates, politicians and other powers of the earth make me feel strangely connected with the qutubs and walis - and with no theories about them.

Thank you,

Shamcher

Dear L__,

It is a pleasure to reply to your letter, even though my reply may be a shock or a disappointment to you. For I cannot give you a straight line onto perfection. Generally, the present state of humanity is immature, testing, seeking, including all branches of science, literature, religion, but there is tremendous potential. A few individual physicists, and yogis and sufis seem to be somewhat ahead, nevertheless, I cannot recommend you to join any of them. I would think it would be fine to join a sufi or yoga group if you understand that most of your co-students (including the "big" teachers) are as yet searching, like yourself. Looking around I can recognize only one safe yoga teacher and perhaps two different sufi teachers, the two brothers Pir Vilayat and Hidayat Khan. They have different organizations because they view their father, Inayat Khan's teachings differently. I am a friend of both, argue intensely with both.

While your spiritual path must be free, open and undogmatic, not slavish follower of any teacher, your worldly path should be firm, persistent and, if necessary, dogmatic. I may not be the proper man to say so, for I criss-crossed the globe trying everything for 50 years. Then I studied the Ocean Thermal Difference Energy System in France, brought it to the US, built plants in three sizes at the U. of California. Now giant industries, seven major universities in reports to the National Science Foundation proclaim this the very energy system for the future. My humble "pioneering" had a purpose and has made me a furious protagonist who spends his time hunting down nuclear and oil barons - a life purpose to ease and promote cooperation through ecologically benign technology. Many sufis like to hear about it. Other sufis angrily denounce me being "materialistic," "diluting the message."

My advice: First find what you want to do in the world, always with spiritual ideals softly in the background. Then note and see how much time or energy you can spend on your own or others' spiritual development. Or turn around and join spiritual movements first: That's what some would say, though not I. You are now in the physical world. Meet that one first.

So your questions:

1. Find out what is happening? Only through your physical money-giving work first.

2. Relationship with other humans? No, not always peaceful. Better blazing war if they are resisting what you feel is advance.

3. Control the mind? That is the object of a million years. You do live at least a million years. Yoga and sufi can teach you, through breathing and concentration.

4. Retain, hold down a steady job? Steady is not the criterion, but useful.

5. Fight off despair, depression? The previous items will take care of that. No need for any despair, depression.

6. Find joy, love? Yes, mainly through the above measures.

7. Become a complete man? In a sense you are already. In another sense that is the ultimate goal.

Love,

Shamcher

This one letter of course is just a drop. Come on again, shall we sing together?

Dear M__,

This is to state you don't need, shouldn't even try, to get a guru-master-teacher yet, until you have utilized the amazing fact that once upon a time you learned to decipher hieroglyphics we call letters - even words, concepts and sentences.

So you buy from Swami Rama's Himalayan Institute his book *Lectures on Yoga* and read from page 71 and on about concentration. The whole book is about concentration, so don't miss all the other parts. It is the kind of book you can read again and again and each new reading you say, "By golly, I didn't see this last time - this mysterious book gives me a whole new picture every time I read it."

I have been reading this every morning from 6:35 to 6:50 waiting for my ride to work. Up at 4:00 doing meditation, I should say dabbling in meditation and physical and mental exercises, breathing, eating a bit of fruit, the morning goes quickly until my ride comes. The book costs about $2.60. I have only got two now, end of pay period. I exchange it occasionally for another precious book of his, *Ishopanishad, The Book of Wisdom*. Amazing I didn't catch this before. That you could read. You can, don't you? No use disturbing the swami until you have read these two books of his five times. Tell me how you feel about them, how easy it is for you to read them. That will tell me more about you. Not about the books, they are tops. I have never read anything more concise, useful, informative, well-organized.

Love, and apology for not having hit on this before,

Shamcher

Dear R___,

You are so beautifully fulfilling all expectations of your reaction to our actions or words. There might be a moment's fear: Would it be considered intruding? Right away comes your reassuring response: Gadfly. Don't panic - Socrates was also called a Gadfly. Actually the word means *God*-fly, a fly in which almighty God himself has taken abode. But in Webster's dictionary it says: a fly who stings horses. No no. I do not sting horses but I may sting men who whip horses, of their own mind, which has been described in yoga lore as, "four horses galloping in all different directions. . ."

No, I don't say transfer your loyalty. No, I don't say that, but that the time may soon come when you transfer your loyalty to the *gadfly*, or God within yourself and look out with love and discrimination upon all your fellowmen. Oh, yes, we talked of all this - organizations, and hierarchies, and how Inayat Khan in his last years laughed at what he himself had written a few years before. And how much more efficient are non-hierarchical organizations - with a deeper finer hierarchy: found inside each individual, not outside, not in the titles. But now where does all this lead you, us? To health, individually, collectively, and efficiency and freedom.

Incidentally, there are no "successors" ever.

Love,

Shamcher

December 10, 1976

Dearest Shamcher,

We have been snowed in for a few days this week. Living in country but still tied to the city there are many disadvantages. But it is so very healing to be here.

The book: I am still working on it and really the most work of it for me is getting through the aspects of myself that stop me from doing it. My shyness (and pride) getting in the way. While pregnant with Rosie, headwork was impossible. Now the way seemed clear for me to forge ahead (its about 1/3 done) and my typewriter is out of ribbon, we were snowed in, etc. etc. Typing the old letters is lesson upon lesson to me - what an amazing process.

I am concerned with a phenomenon for which I feel somehow responsible: it seems that many people I connect clearly with tend to be a little unstable or nutty and contact with me seems to be a somewhat disruptive force. Not that I'm doing anything at all, but when I look back I wonder if you know of anything I can do - can I explain? I was close with one and she lost all grip on "reality" - though she was so before. Then another, so totally paranoid and so beautiful. Then someone else flashing violently from open to closed. Now another friend is in a mental institution here, and I heard another went away and had a breakdown. I feel somehow like I could have helped in some way. The mind and heart are so fragile in us really. We are all seeking "sanity", though it's not what we think we're looking for.

Of course, I can think of all those with whom I am close who are not so unstable, but knowing people deeply, becoming them, I become totally involved.

This letter feels like a searching letter, a groping towards the opening which I feel is immanent. To say to you I love you and am so grateful is part of the doorway's opening. The other part is letting go of the censor in me to tell you that my life is entirely changed and it is through you and all those whom you channel that this marvel began to awaken and change me. I can look back with greater understanding and look forward without fear. And this present is a crystalline marvel beyond compare. The mystery of the one we keep hidden is a forever unfoldment of awe.

And although I have so often been covered, I still can shine whenever needed, whenever called. This is the marvelous paradox of *me* or is it me? Or is it so indefinable that it isn't possible in words? This miraculous fountain shows higher and higher its splendid waterforms, and with each splash comes a new understanding in my heart. It was you who showed me the key to this flood of light and love. Now the fountain sustains me, and when I ask within an answer always comes if I have ears to hear. Yet if I were totally self-sufficient, it would only give me enough capacity to love your total being as you actually deserve. I know that I'm endowing you with all powers and all wonders. Yet you do this with me, and in this atmosphere comes what is needed. To see you would give my heart great joy! To be near you - but to do what is best for you is always what I must consider.

Remember this, dearest one, our time together now is very short, and there is more transfer needed for I'm not at all grounded. The need is for broader experience in order to cope with the needs of those who contact me.

They don't want me, "Carol", they want themselves, and I must learn to be clear enough to shine without self. In this I still need your help, for there are earth-parts holding me. But then I flash so easily from big self to little self, depending on my attention focus. I have no way of speaking such things, but it is all I really have to say.

Except this - you are forever the finest being on earth to me and a precious one - I would do anything for you, use me in any way you can and I promise I will not fail you. It's so confusing here for the voice of this pen is you, me, beyond us both and so applies to you, me and beyond with each stroke.

Merry Christmas,
Carol

December 17, 1976

Dear Carol,

Every letter from you is entirely new and more delightful than any of the previous ones. When I think you cannot go higher, oh yes, higher and deeper and more true ever you go.

Since I may not be able to keep up with this pace, I just enclose some copies showing what I am up to. As you see I tell both about the stage most of us are on but should perhaps have mentioned that there are beings all the way to the top? But wouldn't that awake their resentment?

Carol, you are so precious and I am also longing to see you. No plans crystallized yet. Awaiting phone calls from various quarters. Unable to plan. Just roll with the punches, as they say in the U.S.

Love, Carol, Love
double and double,
Shamcher
P.S. Yes, will be "retired" 31 December. Had colossal party, gold watch, (and it even runs, and correct) brief case, plaque, despite my efforts to prevent party.

P.S. When people you connect with are nutty or unstable (who isn't?) be proud that you were found worthy of helping, guiding them - and don't think *you* are, but through your mere presence great beings descend upon them and do the necessary - which may not always be much, at this moment. "Explain?" Not necessary. If anything comes to mind, say it. I always work against institutionalizing, for it is immature as yet, but when you are overpowered by other factors, let go, don't worry any longer. But spread your love, it is magnificent and more.

Dear D__,

Your ambition toward your own version of "perfection" is proof that you are on your way and will arrive. One day you will discover that there is no "God" outside of or separate from yourself and your ideas. Your ideas are God's ideas at this stage of your journey. To blame yourself (God) for not doing to you what you think (now) he should, will soon appear to you a funny, if not silly thought. And it seems that when you mature, you will make a new heaven and a new earth (and who won't?) according to the brewing already evident. Compare your fate to the specimens who all over the world are placed in torture chambers without the faintest idea of why. They not only suffer pain, they become crippled - in body and mind. What kind of "God" does this? But God is the one who suffers - and the one who inflicts. A hazy aspect of a future God. If you are angry with him, if you consider him a fool and a criminal, go ahead and make a new one. You are expected to. It may take a second or a million years. What is time? An illusion, a human feeling. Sin, you say? What is sin? To sleep with a woman? Man has two powerful instincts: Survival and progeneration. Hunger is the expression of the former, lust of the other. To you, though, the yogi who never sleeps with a woman except when they want to create a new human being seems a better man. So live accordingly. You can't? But you have not made yourself available to the procedures. That is why I sent you where you could have discovered that even an imperfect woman could have given you breathing exercises that would make it possible for you to concentrate. Are you doing the one nostril - the other nostril breathing in the morning? If this is necessary for concentration why do not the schools teach it? HaHaHa. The schools are simply an extension of our collective foolishness, immaturity. Then I sent you to someone else; that you didn't stick with him can only be credited to your foolishness. Nowhere in the world can you get better instruction. You didn't like him? What does he care, or I!

If you like, you may think of many lives, through which after a million years you reach *God*. But you may be far ahead on those million years, maybe three years only to go.

Love,

Shamcher

Dear R___,

It appears to me you demand instant wisdom now. And instant results now or thirty seconds ago. Did I too, when I was your age? I cannot recall. But now, at 80, I expect almost nothing of my fellowmen, including the "Teachers." Indeed I consider it a felony or at least a misdemeanor to call oneself a teacher. Most pupils who have taken their teachers seriously are deplorably shallow - for that reason. You hear them parrot some dogma - and teaching in their turn.

Humanity today, including all branches of science and a great deal of yoga and sufism, is on a primitive, immature stage. Physical scientists, some of them, are, like some yogis, a bit further advanced.

I think when you get rid of your high horse demanding instant flex, you may progress rather nicely toward whatever is your goal and which shouldn't be anybody else's. I can't for the life of me see why you cannot admit that the aspect of God that is you is as yet a whining, frustrated beginner on the path of life. If you were perfect, why the hell were you born here? No reason. You were born to learn. Why do you think you, of all people, would be born finished? I swarmed all over the globe looking, not for a solution, but for a beginning. Why do you expect it to happen on a farm? But it may. In that case be thankful.

"God is almighty," shouts the simple. Trash. From the point of view of all time, yes, because there is nothing else he, you, I can be. But at this time: a helpless child. Now go to the task, by golly, without whining. You don't want to stumble or falter? Like everybody else? Ah, what conceit, what incredible pride, what economy: you don't want to falter. While the society around you is doing nothing else, all the time, in energy, in economics. These revealing aspects of the spirit, in war technology. And you, you want to be an untouchable elite high above the scum. Well, I am shouting pretty nastily at the scum right now, since it is a bit worse, I think, even than myself. But I am shouting myself hoarse, with no joy. But with vigor, a vigor borrowed from God.

And incidentally you have poured acid on me all the time without even trying the few little exercises I gave. Life is nothing without continuous exercises. Thoughts are childish. Exercises help thoughts becoming transfixed, changed altogether.

Love,
Shamcher

1977
THE ANSWERS ARE IN THE QUESTIONS

When Inayat Khan first met me he was delighted to have a Lao Tzu man in his message, knowing all along my endless record, knowing that I would initiate and pursue the formless, like you and so many.

Shamcher

January 7, 1977

Dearest Carol,

I have been so touched by you and your friends' appeal to come to Stony Plain. I have a "roving appointment" with a personage in January, so can't leave then. And after that, isn't it regularly so much snow in your place that one may anytime be snowed in at the airport and never come any further? And you can't come to the airport? Otherwise we might have sufi dancing and singing and hulabaloo at the airport, to the great entertainment of all those others snowed in. And what about March? And half of April? But here we are always happy to see Christmas-heaven-god-the best friends show up and locate them in convenient motels.

I am so happy, Carol, to have the opportunity of communicating with you again, though such a shallow letter.

Love,

Shamcher

January 10, 1977

Dearest Shamcher,

Thanks so for all the newsclippings of you - it was great to see your smiling face come out of the envelope! And as to your letter - if fear of being snowed in is your real reason for not coming for a while, let me sweep it away in a flash - it rarely, if ever, happens. The road to the airport is always made clear and I could pick you up and it would be easy. We were snowed in here on the land, but that was before the grader came in to clear it.

The truth (if I can say this) of the understanding of no one earthly teacher is coming clearer and clearer to me as all I am close to teach me so much. Each person carries innumerable lessons, each instant holds opportunities. The only limitation to this learning is in myself - each person I meet holds a key to open another of my locks - and how the soaring changes from being to being. I am so grateful. Isn't it marvelous - this circulation of deep life within all?

Love, love, love,

Carol

January 15, 1977

Dear Carol,

If you still want a visit from this indistinguished and unworthy person, it now looks like a faint possibility after the 21st, when I am supposed to appear here in Seattle (I mean, in near-by Seattle.) Whether circumstances blow our way after that I don't know yet. We'll see.

Meanwhile you have a *Planet Earth Demands* copy? And will you most kindly quote to me the first line of the first chapter, plus the first line on page 27? This will show me whether you have the latest corrected issue. Very important to me.

A woman at the Harvard Undergraduate Press became very interested in "The Message" in the book but flatly states that it has to be rewritten. From enclosed copy of my letter to her, you'll see high-hatted me taking a stand, yet offering her tentatively to try. You of course could do it much better. But you have so many other things to do, you probably haven't yet even finished your own letter-book? Now tell me very frankly what you think of her remarks, my answer and the book *Planet Earth Demands*.

Love, universes, books, hearts,

Shamcher

January 23, 1977

Dear Carol,

Your sparkling letter, sparkling with the spirit, with love, with realization - thank you. I have only one regret now: Your next to last letter, only a quarter of a page, with a most significant "wide" in it - I cannot find, so cannot return, for the book - or is that too late anyway? The book of letters has gone to the publisher? So I can read it all over again? Treasure it on my shelf?

Yes, after your last letter my trip to Edmonton has came much closer. I owe a trip to the Bay area, for business (unpaid, of course, may even cost more, but later maybe return) and friends, and hope soon to make it to Edmonton or a little beyond, But a pity thinking of you driving that long way to the airport. Maybe I could take a limosine?

Everybody seems to gather at 567 Stony Plain. I have letters from L__, from J___, from God and his Grandmother.

Your words in regards to all those pictures in the papers are so funny. I sent you the clippings to remind you how awful I look. Do you really want such a one at beautiful Stony Plain? Might burn a hole in the walls. I was asked by the present leader of the Khankah in Seattle to inaugurate the season with a talk. I said one thing initiations may do is clean up one's spiritual companionship - seen and unseen beings who flock around one. But an exchange of glances can do the same. "Does one need a teacher?" No, except that some want one. But you need company, association, and I mentioned some examples I had seen of people who tried complete solitude - how very talkative they became because. . . I talked about the five ships, the five vehicles of sufi line and that one of them, the order, was the most important for many of us because it provides training: Practices, that change mind, personality, the only thing that can change it besides love. I rambled around worse than ever and they sat there in their perfect yoga postures and pretended there was nothing wrong.

Love,

Shamcher

This week I have a video on Thursday so...

February 14, 1977

Dear Carol.

Having always looked down on those Canadian mountains with longing from an airplane, I fancied I would come as an earth worm this time, so I have troubled bus and rail and come to choose a possible rail from Vancouver starting 8:30 mornings and arriving Edmonton (rail station) 10 at night or so and that would be below your bedtime so you must tell me of a cheap-cheap-cheap hotel in Edmonton where I can sleep to meet you in the morn bright.

Yes, I need to come to Edmonton now for that wonderful dentist the mentist who put in a tooth-top - it lasted till yesterday - what is 1.5 or 2 years? While my Silverdale dentist's top never lasted more than 4 days - whether because he wanted to encourage me to tear them all out and have one of his awful plates instead I never knew. In Canada they don't have such schemes.

A British doc visiting New York was asked why British docs were so respected while Americans were not. "Perhaps," he said, "Because we usually try to heal our patients, while you American doctors are too busy with your investments to try that." Oh yes, and I found these fine proposals of Ahmed? By all means, do it. Excellent.

Carol. How I love you - all of you ...

Shamcher

March 14, 1977

Dear Carol,

Yes, I am home again after a luxurious trip on the CN. Please thank extravagantly all the beautiful people treating me so undeservedly wonderful in Edmonton-Stony Plain, Gary, Lody, John, Diane, Bill I and Bill II, in whose latter house I slept like a log and in whose former I said so many silly things, Latif, the savior and drill sergeant, Ahmed the inspired, all those youngsters being so far ahead of me.

You see, I am so important now I have four (4) names on my envelope so I can really see and enjoy my importance - or are they there to conceal some awful secret underneath? Enclosed page 27 for *Planet Earth*. Will you please send me express Airmail report that this has been received and placed into the book in lieu of the old one - to jittery, fragile li'l Shamcher?
Love and longing for Edmonton,
Shamcher

March 16, 1977

Dear Shamcher,

What can I say about your fine visit here? How can I ever thank you for coming? We have decided to move from this place back to the city. What a strange turn of circumstances. And just when friends said to me, "We're going to move out to the land this summer." I had to say, "Great, but we won't be there, we're moving back to the city." Any comments? I feel so totally buffeted by all the cross-currents that I can't tell whether I am coming or going or here at all!!!!

One day I am so fragile that all experience makes me quiver, and the next I feel almost solid. I am smashed open again, exposed and vulnerable, swimming in new waters entirely. What I used to think was it - all my notions which were formed and built up, unworded but present - all this has crashed to the ground, leaving a gap. Really, it's as if all that I thought is gone, leaving me in a strange state indeed. Now I feel the new concepts forming, not the same as before. So you left this wake behind you. I feel totally changed - but the same. What can I say anymore about anything at all?

It was so beautiful to be with you, especially in those moments we shared together alone in the universe. Last night at sufi dancing I thought, "Why am I doing this? It is so far from what could be done," and then I just threw myself into it, doing it wholeheartedly. I think the time has come that

171

I can no longer word my experience at all, and there is no way to express on paper the depth and breadth of this world of love. I must be silent on that, and simply express instead my eternal gratitude to you for all you are, and my deepest thanks for your coming here, for such a short time you traveled so far.

The changes in all you met are so apparent to me. The last time you were here it was much gentler, but this time there were strong changes. So I saw you appear as an angel and as a devil (to some) and in all forms, the only thing to be said is strong and uncompromising and this has shaken me for I realized that I'm always smoothing feathers and making calm, sometimes at the expense of the expression that is needed at the time.

We will keep the light shining in whatever ways we can.

Love,

Carol

And more: It seems that I should meet more people and see different viewpoints if I am to help the sufis at all. I want to meet others, just for the contact. At the same time I must clear myself further. There is a new world opening up for me and I'm so small in it and there is so much that I want to let go of to *be* this new world. I am nothing at all. It is all so vast, and I know nothing, how can I even be worthy to serve? But it has little to do with me anyways, I act when I must and do as I must, that is all.

March 23, 1977

Dear Shamcher,

How fine to hear from you again. We are looking for a house to live in, in the city. It seems more than right. Our life is changing radically on the outside, yet it feels sort of dreamlike and somehow unreal, but real of course. A reflection, I suppose, of the inner changes, whatever they may be. And Ahmed gave me his robe which he uses for his prayers.

Please write and tell me of the leaders seminar and what it was and how it went and all. I don't feel that I should have been there, but perhaps at the next one.

It's as if I hold within me some small clear light which can be described as the root of truth - this will never change despite all the changing forms around it. And as it isn't dependent upon anything, it has only to be and the world is transformed with each breath. But why do things get always messed up and organized and be-laboured until the light is seemingly extinguished?

Oh, I give you a true smile and a big hug.

Love forever,

Carol

March 29, 1977

Yes, lovely queen of Alberta and the North Pole, I knew you were moving to town again, and it is good, just like your great days in the lovely outdoors were good and lovely, a real experience.

Right: No changes should be lasting, all is further change. I do not myself realize that I was gentler before or stronger after, what does it mean?

Yes, the leaders camp was interesting and I had a long talk with Vilayat explaining how I must also work for Hidayat. It is just that I want Vilayat always to stay on top in his present position and carry on as he thinks best, which gives him his strength as his father wishes. But I do not usually go to camps so if you are going sometime and wish me to be there, you better phone in advance, and would it be lovely to meet you again, Carol! After camp I went to New Orleans for the fourth OTEC workshop and battled long and fiercely along with other stalwarts. A man from congress' Office of Technologic Assessments was there and showed that this office had fallen neatly into a trap I warned against 9 months ago, and we'll see what we can do about it.

As usual, I send you back your precious letters, but now I suppose your book is finished, besides, these letters are mainly practical things, not much on the subtler lovable things, though partly they are - you use your judgement and please, get this book out - in Canada. Four sufis in New York are now creating a publishing house with the first task of publishing my books - *Fairy Tales are True* or *Every Willing Hand* first, then all the others. But your book, I hope, will be published by a Canadian, not a U.S. publisher, and you touch the beautiful, essential evanescent *truth* with yours, which nothing can match. No, yes, some in your enclosed letters are sensational - really worth including

Oh Carol something funny happened to me on my way to the OTECS workshop: I found out that I love you! Again!

Shamcher

And what about those Indian songs?

March Newsletter
PRE-URS

I am way behind schedule. Forgive me please. Urs was twenty-three days ago and here I am still fumbling with Pre-Urs, to be exact: Four days before the first Urs.

I was living in Norway, three days by ship and rail to Suresnes, the sufi Summer School. This was not Summer but mid-winter, Norwegian style, big boots, heavy coats and mufflers. Yet, an untimely, unseemly urge told me to go to Suresnes. I cussed myself, scolded myself, tried to restrain myself; nothing helped. On the steamer my eye hurt. I could not see. Serves you right, I thought, going to summer school in mid-winter. The ship called at Stavanger. I saw an eye doctor who pulled out a hair.

In Suresnes, to my surprise, others had come too, from all over Europe and even from America. All of them were just as surprised, as disgusted as myself. None of us had any explanation for our irresponsible behavior.

At five in the morning February 5th, there was a message. Pir-O-Murshid Inayat Khan, then in India, had passed over to the other world. We, chumps, who had gathered in Suresnes for no apparent reason were now in charge of the message. I recalled my last meeting with Inayat Khan 26 September, 1926. I said to him, "I am looking forward to seeing you next summer." "From now on, Shamcher, you will meet me in your intuition."

Intuition?

Was that what had driven us all to Suresnes that winter?

For some, their "intuition" went a bit further and played tricks on them. They came forward, one after another, the following days, claiming to have been appointed the leader, the "successor," some even by a message from Inayat Khan "through a medium," although Inayat Khan had spent the four last speaking hours of his life to warn us that a teacher never speaks to a pupil "through a medium." We chose the one least eager or willing to be the leader, the successor: Maheboob Khan, Inayat's brother - to take charge until Vilayat would be of age.
Shamcher

April 4, 1977

Dear dear Carol,

Continuing renewal and revising as time requires, here comes a new page 6a to be substituted for the old page 6a in *Planet Earth Demands*, and the old page should and must hurriedly be burned or cannibalized or eliminated so it does not turn up again and confuse the poor reader. Thank you, Carol, and my apology. Do you have the script *Every Willing Hand* too? Then I must send you a different new page for that.

Why do I begin with such dry, crackling wood? Instead of saying, Oh, Carol you are not merely heavenly, you contain within you heaven and earth and all the things and beings on and in and within and without them.

And now you are publishing the book that will lift the spiritual-emotional-mental world to viability. What did your publisher say? Or is it still awaiting dispatch? You know, I have gotten myself a publisher in New York and now a film maker is hurrying a book-film scenario involving OTECS and bureaucrats and company hags and hacks and the whole world of excitement. Which will be first? You?

An energy workshop in San Francisco 2 August featured a good film by Lockheed (11 minutes) not the kind described above but good in its type. Also one of the first critical and attempting to be damning talk on OTECS by a utility man. Easy to answer. But when or who will get a chance to answer?

I wrote Pir Vilayat, congratulating him on the clear and beautiful piece in *The Message*. A "resignation" means breaking an initiation tie that was supposed to last at least a lifetime, from the side of the mureed as well as the teacher. But, I said, your own earlier suggestion of a dervish order on the side of the Sufi Order of people strongly wishing to help the message but not fitting into the order may do. Plus a six months "actualization" period in which these things are worked out. But over and above such tactics or strategy comes your Canadian line that we have worked out and are working out so beautifully, and you are right to ask how should we do it - and I am right in doing nothing final now but see how it will naturally develop under our compassionate care, as time goes on.

Love, Carol, and love,

Shamcher

April 11, 1977

Dear Carol,

Your most precious letter of April 5, of course you are lost, who isn't if he/she is honest? You are dying, for the thousandth time, and finding the true life (being nothing yourself, no self) for the 1001 times. And look how lucky you are, so happy you can be, in being the non-participating leader just because you know nothing. What do you think I am to all the sufi centres - they don't even know I exist (and I am certainly not telling them) except that a lone seeker suddenly phones me, "Shamcher, what is it all about? There is Idries Shah, he seems so firm and absolute, he seems to really have something while we are just playing, aren't we?" "Yes, and play on! You deserve it!" "But Shamcher, I want to be Zen, there is where I really belong." "Of course, that is your play - now." "But is there nothing else than play?" "Call it sweat if you like. It is all about crawling or sprinting toward your goal - humanity's goal." "But what is it, that goal?" "You'll find out. If you knew it all now, why strive? Besides, about Zen: one of the finest most energetic Edmonton Canada members of the sufi effort is a Zen and a university teacher of Zen."

Carol: You need do nothing. A "leader" who impresses his own personality is all wrong. Lead by doing nothing (at first) but see. See and admire and rest - until one day you might find expression to your longing for the "deeper" - and present it, at any meeting - and perhaps meet great resistance - or applause, what does it matter? I asked for and had a long interview with Pir Vilayat in San Francisco trying to impress upon him that you must always remain the leader there, and after your letter I am even more sure.

We have both made serious mistakes of course, and I am excited and happy to discover our mistakes.

I am also funds-poor now, no more travel opportunity than you, and this gives me a chance to work better. I am grateful for it, and I use it as an excuse to all who try to command my presence in far corners. Carol: you are doing wonderfully. This may seem easy for me to say, who already know all the sufis (no not all) and who has travelled and whom everybody calls upon as the greatest authority. But you have it all without all this travel and apparent knowledge. So what're you bawling about? Your letter is wonderful.

You could start Universal Worship? Once, twice a month? If you wish, if many wish. Stress the message of *Freedom*.
Love,
Shamcher

April 12, 1977

Dear Carol,

I wake up, frantic! I went all that way to Stony Plain and missed the chief reason I was called there!!!!

What was it? That chief reason? Oh Carol, please help.
Your fatally loving,
Shamcher

April 15, 1977

Oh dearest Shamcher,

    Your last two letters have almost shattered my already shattered heart and what now can I ever say? First - you felt you missed the reason for coming to Stony Plain? Well, when you left I felt the sense of incompleteness, but since that time so much has changed in the wake of your visit that I am sure you completed your task here. But if not, come back!

    Remember this - I will do whatever I can to further this effort, and here in Edmonton is a perfect opportunity for uniting many seemingly diverse forces. Even now are plans for a meditation centre, where Buddhists, and Native Indians and sufis and who knows who else will all come into the essential oneness. Oh if only there were the clarity. Yet in the glimpses, in the attempt, this is enough.

    I ride the stream of love which is your unfathomable being.
Carol
About the Indian songs - I believe the sacred songs of power are never recorded. Tell the person to come here and take part in a sweat and hear them for real.

April 15, 1977

Dear Carol,

    Of course you are 5/4 angel and 2/4 geni so it's only right that you should trek with the angels and that is why you are so irresistible and so well-suited as leader of the sufis in Edmonton. However, your 2/4 geni assures you a place in the television and literary world. Of course, you are physical too. So your physical and geni world pulls your angels down to earth and shows them to the amazed world. But hurry. It is never too early. No, Carol, the flame doesn't burn you. That's the difference between the physical fire and the angel's fire. Indeed, physical fire doesn't burn the subtler things either, nor does the subtler fire or flame burn anything at all. What do you think fire walkers are and do?

    But get that book out or you may feel another kind of fire.

    But I haven't talked or written quite rightly now, I haven't gotten into your beautiful spirit, for I am not now as much angel as you are, too deeply involved in OTECS, economics and all that (and I have to be, as ordered, commanded to be.) So all I can say with my little limited self I love you, to all my limited ability - oh, it isn't so damned limited after all. I find I love you a lot, why I am not limited at all!! So there! Not limited in love to you anyway.

Love,

Shamcher

April 16, 1977

Carol, what are you talking about? YOU, who have a million-dollar book ready? Or isn't it ready? Shame on you, wasting your time like that.

Type, woman, type! And also you are supposed to, destined to bring out the greatest sufi tradition, the typically Canadian one, engineered by yourself and a damned US foreigner and immigrant, don't you remember? Look at me with my inferior mind: I have already created a publishing house here, now you can at least create a book there!

Carol, don't procrastinate any longer but tell me in your next letter that the book is being printed NOW.

Good morning Carol, and have a good day and a better evening.

Love,

Shamcher

May 3, 1977

Dear Shamcher,

Although I said I wouldn't write to you until the letters were all typed, here I am unable to keep away, typing the past, while there is so much present. We have moved to the city again and we are presently staying at B__'s house. Life is so rich and full since coming back into the city - deep relationships and fine feelings. We don't have a place to live permanently yet, but this is fine for now. Gary just got a flood of work writing music for educational television, so we will soon have a bit more money too,

But lost is the best word for now, and opening to all the newness that can never be described. Please write to me when you can.

In a way I feel closer to you while typing the letters, but to see you would be even better. I'd like to go to the Toronto camp, as you will be there, and I could meet those people and share being, get a better understanding of

178

the approach they take, etc. but Toronto is very far away and it would be too expensive a trip. So give them my love when you go.

Last night at Gatha class I found that I couldn't read as prescribed, when I began to read I knew that I couldn't do it, and put the paper down and began to talk instead, to say that the papers are appropriate for certain situations, but not that particular one. We had silence, and then I talked for a time. It was so very remarkable not because of what was being said, but rather because of the energy or power or feeling through the room, and in my being. I have never known anything quite so fine and exquisite and yet so powerful at the same time.

My mind is just flying around as there is much to tell you but I can't catch the rhythm as yet. It's easier for me to open in all ways now, at the slightest hint I dive in and am gone completely - what is this about? How best can we create and recreate and regenerate the world in this way? Whatever I must do, I do without hesitation, or if there is hesitation, then I go through as best I can. Like now: there is a slight hesitation, it's difficult to express some of the deeper ones in faithfulness. Best to let it remain unsaid, except for this: the way we work and how we send our finest expressions is through deep and unrelenting beams of purest love. The entire universe is so very alive all seen and unseen, so very vibrant and sparkling – how do we channel this deep mystery within and through our little finite beings? By moving over and letting the beams flow through directly without hindrance. To you, Shamcher, I can shine more than with anyone, for you are so far above - your being allows so much to pass through unhindered. I'm a baby taking first steps, and I see you fly above me through the sky.

Your star and mine are one, and this is why our connection is true and deep. In that radiant star that we are, beyond this, we shine and create all things new, and totally without word, touch, sight, or even differentiation. And in the realm of the stars, we shine and join with all other great star-beings to form triads and patterns of infinite beauty, flickering for only an instant. Now to translate this to the grosser earth part is not as difficult as it might seem, for the unity is already fait accompli, and it is only a matter of time. I love you forever.
Carol

May 16, 1977

Dear Carol,

I ought to go into a special sacred holy room when writing to you; it is a mission. Your letter again was fresh and new like morning dew. I return it to you so you may include it in your holy script.

From July on I will live in Berkeley-Richmond in California, being from then on a research-associate at the university until the end of 1977. In June I will be travelling: Washington, New York, New Hampshire and the Canadian Camp in Toronto. For the first time in my life I will have to accept part of my travelling expenses from Toronto, where by the way, they charge for the camp so I do not take from anyone person but from all. A shame. Or perhaps good. It is really a hard decision: Should I not come at all and keep my independence and at the same time remain anonymous? I don't know. But the decision seems to be: Going, going, gone. It may turn out a surrender or it may turn out a flaming inferno.

You know, Carol, I am not not not going into detail about what you might do, for you are far ahead of me both as a person and as a knower of the Alberta trend. I know know know that whatever you do or don't is right right right. And that you will be moved by greater spirits than mine, by your exquisite team around you. Therefore and for a billion other reasons and for no reasons I love you.
Shamcher

May 17, 1977

Dear D__,

Thank you for your beautiful letter. Yes, your "sacrifice" may be just that. To stay in the city while you yearn to flee to the country. Even wishing to die I have felt so often, but never as a wish to break off myself. But in World War II I volunteered for the most crazy suicide missions almost hoping to never come back, but I came back healthier than ever. Our chief physician said, "Bryn, you are the first I have observed who seems to have no nerves, no fear." But actually I had fear, not of death, but of pain, the transition.

No, I have a profession, but does that help me any? I have gone through just as many silly routine jobs as you. Only once did my engineering make sense: when I worked on Ocean Thermal Energy Conversion at the University of California, having taken this system with me from my studies in France. But I did not know at that time how important this was and now is.

Your thoughts and feelings have their effects on the whole humanity so you needn't worry about spilt time. Nothing is spilt. Inayat Khan would have said, and did say, "Why don't you join my noble effort, man?" and 'man' would reply, "No, I want to be free." "Oh?" said Inayat, "You want to be free? But man, you aren't. For you are afraid of me and my school. But I am free. For I am not afraid. I go bouncing around all day and night for my friends, and that's what makes me free." At Inayat's time we often starved working for sufism. Nowadays nobody starves and many get rich. It is an easier time. You could go into only sufi work if you wish. Or, like me, keep a touch with all and every thing and kind. Oh yes every sufi group has good translations of the *Koran*, Carol has. But *Gayan, Vadan and Nirtan* are better for today. And *Soul, Whence and Whither*. Summary of Bucke: All good except age. Illumination takes place at all ages for everybody. He is a bit static. All beginners are. Yes, of course "prayer" or meditation helps.
Love,
Shamcher

June 1, 1977

Dear Shamcher,

Something I want to share with you: We were planning the first of our regular Universal Worship services and were looking through books to find readings – suddenly came this beautiful idea: if we were to substitute "Jesus" or "Christ" for "Atman" and "God" for "Brahman" . . . and we did, reading aloud with this substitution, and . . . it was so true we could barely breathe! Not only was it the same voice and the same words (sometimes it seemed word for word from the Bible) but we found a much more clear idea of who Christ was/is. For me it was a confirmation and a blessing - a definite encouragement for Universal Worship. The service, by the way, was beautiful, and a Tibetan Lama who lives here came and spoke about the unity of religions.

Ever since moving back to town, life has accellerated beautifully, there is much more going on organizationally with the sufis, and between people it is also deeper. It seems that I am always with people and there seems little time to myself anymore. Who am I anyways? It will even out.

Last week Gatha class was deep and very strong. I felt a depth unknown before and when it was done, such a yearning to be alone and absorb it all or to keep a stillness, but instead I was thrown into activities, looking after

Rosie, doing the diaper wash, driving the car, when all of me was gone. I am asking should I even yearn for this still time or should I just throw myself into whatever is going on at the time? I don't think I resent the ties that pull me back to earth, but is it indulgence to yearn for such a time of stillness? It was hours before I could carry on normally, though from the outside it seemed that I was just quiet. From Gathas and from Universal Worship I see that my rhythm is so much faster than the rhythm of that sphere and I must slow down.

We're planning a weekend of practices and dancing and such in June - people want to get together and do something.

One thing I've found difficult being back in town is seeing people so much and having people in love with me and me with them - I tell them its not me, what can I do? And people want to be with me but I also need time alone. There have been just continuous streams of visitors - all dear friends, but what about Rosie and Gary? And what about myself? Perhaps it will be different when the initial rush from the move back to Edmonton is over, then I hope things will settle down to a more regular rhythm.

I know that my main learning takes place now in Gatha and Universal Worship, for here the reflection of Inayat Khan is so deeply felt, and I have never known anything like it. Do I then stay in the state created by this, by closeting myself away for a time after, or do I instead dive into the world and all the relationships and just pour it all into all by doing? Or does this drain away power? The other day the thought came to me after meditation: I am a maker of perfume, and the perfume-making has just begun in me.

Love,

Carol

This writing came the same night -

Impatient with the media through which I contact that marvelous inspirational source - all these means seem flat and lifeless to me. I need wider scope, broader means by which to create and destroy forever realms upon realms - to include the dimensions of feeling and thought - to evolve the total perfect consciousness - to give and give and give forever that this perfect consciousness may be made manifest and to sing of this manifestation - to imply by symbols entire worlds, to live simply and without impediment, to laugh lovingly with the world and to cry without stop through the smiles. I seek a human form to express all that I am, and this human can begin to approximate my life on earth. I seek humanity as a whole to come together in oneness that it may approximate my union in being.

I seek God and God alone.

Now it can be clearly seen and understood that this writing is perhaps your clearest tool. Let this be the lesson: do the best you can and all things will be added as you need them. We speak of trust as one of our most treasured qualities. Also faith and love, forever kindled.

June 21, 1977

Beloved Carol,

Filled to the top of my attic with abject love for that queen of the North Pole and Edmonton - you know - I came home to a rainbow shooting out of a pot of gold and sinking into another pot of gold, from that same queen. And she asked, might she go out into solitude whenever she so felt or would this be wrong? That queen is always entitled to go out into the woods and solitude when she so feels, it is her birthright. Although she is strong enough not to go if she feels duty binds her. She is free to go or not to go. It is good.

And the camp was good for it whole-heartedly accepted you - and even me. And it rained.

And "The Strangers" was good especially when it came to Fa-Mun-Ji, the Chinese scientist who wrote his son in 1270 AD: "Here the empire has collapsed. The soldier is more honored than the scholar, and the scholar relies on his books. The sage shut his door to visitors and goes back to his garden... It was always the teaching of our most honored ancestors that recourse to an oracle was itself a sign of ignorance...It must be understood that the oracle is a pretext...A lame man may use a stick until he recovers the use of his limb. If he relies on the stick too long, he may become deformed. If, once deformed, he bows to the stick, he is in a state of ignorance..."

"...They looked at him as the Doctor Mazimus, yet they could not intuit, beneath his poised and gracious manner, a desperate, almost maddened lover..."

"Said he: when you say of your brother what is true, you have slandered him, and when you say what is not true you have reviled him..."

I return your lovely letter so it may again vibrate your flute and find its place in the Akashic book.

Love,

Shamcher

Talewar Dussac, sufi secretary general under Inayat Khan, often left in the middle of a meeting, "Excuse me, I feel like being with myself, like meditating." Now I am telling the truth about him so I am slandering him. And I am so delighted to read about your activities and that of the others. We knew.

July 4, 1977

Dear Carol,

We are becoming worse than you, holed up in a miniscule apartment to where mail is most uncertain and no room for our useless things in storage in Washington and I received by chance your dear letter in which, however, you use a word I never learned, "sexuality". What is it? Movement without love? To me there is only love, on all places and nothing else. And so, not to hurt those drowned in sexuality, I keep strict limits, but only for their sake, not for any "principle".

Here in California they certainly need me. They are so dumb that they say you cannot park your car anywhere near the university except in day time and I only need to park at night, so I do, taking all the risks, because I have courage, and telling them they need me to organize them and not make silly rules. Either they have to say to a new hire: You can only be hired if you have no car, or - to make arrangement for where he may park, yes, even at night, for we haven't been able to disembody cars at night, at least some of us haven't.

And they need me even more for OTECS. But they don't know yet. Oh Carol, was this a hard and dumb letter? If so, it is because I am hard and dumb. But since I am you, and you are not hard and dumb, I can't be really hard and dumb either, at any rate not for long,
Love,
Shamcher

July 7, 1977

Dearest Shamcher,

Your last letter hit me so hard I really don't know what to say. Something unspoken cut me so deeply and cleanly. When your letter came I was blasted away, just bewildered and so very peaceful and your presence was so strong I could feel you in me, around me and through me. Nothing gives me greater joy than this sweet pain of your presence.

You came with your letter to touch something long forgotten, and you healed and cleansed areas that have been clouded up. I need so to be clear in these understandings so my actions are pure and without blemish. Oh dear dear Shamcher, I wanted to fly right into your arms, and through your body, and into your heart and through forever without a stop.

You know me so well, I only hope to know you as well someday, so I can shine back yourself. To feel your clear power as I did today and as I do right now is so cleansing and fine. It was wordless, it all happened so powerfully wordlessly. And now I feel a million words now ready to burst forth to you.

In the times we now share the work is coming to a beautiful flowering, but to ensure full fruition, discretion in physical life must be observed. It is easy to become carried away by the energies of deep love without feeling fully the impact of action. How can it be clarified when so few know it? Thank you from all of me for your letter - it is too deep for me to say.
Love,
Carol

Oh Shamcher, what have you done to me with your letter? I am melted into a limpid pool, humbled and grateful. You are so swift and clean. Words are too little and even dreams lack dimension to express even 1/8 of this feeling. Give me more of this swift power that cleanses and heals in a glance. The old stuff is burned away, so the true can shine free.

I am more strongly drawn to you than ever before, and dream of you at night. This morning I awoke knowing I had to open this letter to you and add this. Add what? You touched something that I never knew was so in the way. What do I do now? Do I moan around and say I was terrible in my understanding until now and how can I ever ask forgiveness of myself or God or anybody? No. I simply resolve to learn to act rightly and carry on as best as possible. I need you to show me these places for I have habitually learned to ignore them.

Did I feel that I had it made? No, I just couldn't see where to work next. Is it that it never ends, this refinement of being? The paths of this love never become familiar. Last night during zikar I saw everyone I have ever met shining over the entire world as a network of active people revitalizing the earth by shining.

It isn't easy to let go of habitual ways which are comfortable and yet cause pain. To strike out continually for the unknown never letting any brush or clinging vine hold me in one place unchanging, comfortable but not growing anymore - I was in such a place and your letter jolted me from it and called me to be *present* here now, cutting through the overgrown brambles. And now this hidden part has been exposed too and I can begin to uproot it - what a fool I was to think of a separation between love and sex - not to trust sexual expression from fears inherited. The wall between the seeming two was plucked aside and thrown away. Now I'm more confused than ever: without this wall of "principle" then in the closeness of natural contact person to person openly then why don't we express physically? What is the potential pain to others? With each one who has come to me openly, the feeling is strong and pure and true - it could be expressed in innumerable ways. Yet the more I recognize these feelings, the more I see I need not act on them.

It's like a beautiful continuum from heaven to earth with the expressions fine and high to earthly and passionate - all the same. So we choose the fine and high, and choose to resonate there from here - in heart and mind. Yes, we choose. Or do we? It seems that I am learning to be in deep feelings and strong winds and still keep steady in the storm.

You know these waters so much more than I - and are a far more experienced sailor - you even have a good yellow hat!

July 19, 1977

Dear dear Carol,

Your precious double-feature goes right back to its source and book and meanwhile people are coming from the Canada Camp, popping up in Berkeley - oh, you know I live in Berkeley now, 2511 Hearst #103 (94709), working with OTECS at the University of California and your letter is vast and delectable. I enclose some copies showing you how badly I maul my dear friends so maybe you'll spank me.

Carol, everybody loves you, you made such an impression in Canada, one said you were simply phenomenal (aren't you still? It doesn't take a barn to make you phenomenal, does it?) And now, suddenly, the Governor wants to see me. Shall I let him wait? Till I have finished this letter? Or shall I see him now? And write you again later? Which will it be, Carol? OK, I shall see him now. As you say.

So long. Such love. What is it? This love?

Shamcher

July 16, 1977

Dear Shamcher,

You know what? I think I am at last beginning to get ready to begin! Are you going to be at leader's camp at the Abode? I am going to try to make it - why I can't say. It would be so good for me to be with Pir Vilayat for a time, and I want to see how things work in the organization. And if you could go, that would be very good indeed - I'd do whatever I could to get there if you were going.

The times we spend together are so precious in this world, and I feel such a further opening in me since last time we were together, so I am able to love you more fully all the time. How could I possibly shine back even half of your beauty? But you know - all these words now, and when we are together, I am speechless.

You must get so many tales of different experiences, and how do they help? But this one seemed to be a great help, and if you have any comment on it, fine, if not, just let me share the wonder of it. We were chanting and I sensed above my head, extending forever, a thin ladderlike golden tower. It was ladderlike in that it had innumerable levels one on top of the other, and they were all closed with doors shut. Then later in that same evening, suddenly I felt this golden series of levels clearly again, and all the doors of it opened at once, swoosh, forming a clear corridor from somewhere very high above my head. I found I could visualize it at will and it would be there and open. Now the second time it came again and it was open, I found myself not centred in this physical body, but instead I was very tiny and climbing this series of golden levels as a ladder. For some reason I was plucked off the ladder and told it wasn't time yet for me to die, or that I would die if I went further. Now I can feel this ladder of open corridors any time I want to. If I am tired, it pours down light and energy, and if I am distracted, I just open to it and in pours strength.

Rosie just woke up from her nap and I must go. Please write soon and let me know how you are and what is in your heart and mind, and I wish I could see you in person as I do in my heart at this moment.
Love,
Carol

July 17, 1977

Dear Shamcher,

I have this enormous feeling that I must somehow (and I don't know how) learn from you everything I possibly can - and I mean not only information but much more. You can tell me I can look within myself and yes it's all there. But there's a wealth of experience that you carry as your being which I must somehow learn from. Can you help me in this? Is there any way you can tell me more about this? It's not lists that I want, nor is it compilations of facts, nor is it that which I can discover on my own. I wish to share totally in your divine being, to learn through such connection all that cannot be said, and to feel you ever within me. But this is already so. Why do I feel I want more? It's because the time is coming when I will so need your strength - which is also mine, I know - and I feel clearly that you help in ways I haven't even dreamed of. You know, stronger than ever I open myself to you and deeper than ever now I need you. I need you yet am self-sufficient - a strange paradox.

Love,

Carol

July 21, 1977

Dear Carol,

Your golden corridor with the doors open show a very happy state in your person of beautifully symbolizing your path of, what some call, opening of your third eye, (which sees around corners) or, actually, sees and knows without eyes. Note: Not everyone goes this way, it is not a sign of a certain stage. It is a sign of how your specific soul works and informs itself or you. And it is extremely good, especially for a teacher, as long as that teacher does not get the silly idea that he is on a "stage" higher than other stages. When you have reached "enlightenment" there is another further enlightenment waiting for you ahead. No stopping, no final achieving.

Congratulations with that sprout business. Business, you know, is as spiritually rewarding as meditation or chanting and sometimes more. Anyway, one should cultivate all these paths.

Camps? No no, I am not going to any, I have now to concentrate on energy, coming every morning to my lab and waiting for the Governor of California to come here (he has said he would) but I would be overjoyed seeing you anywhere where fate wants us to meet. Yes, you are always

188

welcome to any camp and to acquaintance with other sufis. They always love you. But only if you can really afford it.

Your letter of 17 is simply superb. And the answers are in the questions. When you say all these beautiful things to me, like a baby I laugh and don't quite know to whom you are talking (as Inayat Khan put it.) For I laugh with joy at the beauty of your voice (contents) and I laugh in embarrassment knowing that all these answers are inside you and not in my mind, which hardly exists. But in my soul, which is yours also, it is. And you find it there, as and when you search.

Love,
Shamcher

Dear B__,

Uber allen gipfeln ist ruh
in allen wipfeln spurest du
kaum einen Hauch
Warte nur,
Balde
Ruest du auch.

(Over all mountain tops is stillness / in all the treetops you see / hardly even a falcon / Just wait, / soon / you also will be still.)

Thank you B__, for reminding me of this, that I am already dead, and you too. And my last laugh, about you slouching, and I thought this was silly. No, it isn't silly. Were you at the Canadian sufi camp? Yes, it is difficult to finish a letter or anything because there isn't really any finish. The thing goes on forever and ever. Did you hear Roshi? The tune of the stars? Could you hear them? Could you hear the clapping of two hands? Of one hand? Isn't it marvelous, we have been close together for milleniums and now today we meet for the first time. Do you hear that chatting and banging on the second floor? It is the Roshis, who a hundred years ago entered into eternal silence and have been keeping it up ever since. Can you hear the beautiful sounds of that silence? The screaming and the roaring? Of mute, eternal, unbroken silencium? The three rings. Hallalujah.

A weekend at Santa Cruz and Tuesday Jamiat about drugs and ... In complete silence, a simply roaring in each others ears silence. Such a silence, perfect. Almost and completely.

How not merely incomplete but without even a beginning this letter be. B_, how can I find a beginning? Help, help. What is a beginning? What is complete? Complete? Where are words for this feeling? This will not have to do. It cannot.

Love (page ends but not I)

Shamcher

(written around the page) - A sufi is one who has two points of view, his own and yours.

August 7, 1977

Dear dear Shamcher,

Isn't it that the greater the intimacy, the less and less personal the contact? But you go through the impersonal to the personal to the intimacy - personally I like to see from the inside out.

More than ever now I am one with you and in a sense the vanguard of your work (and mine and all) forward into a new form with broader field of action and richer experience - no separation between "sufism" and life - oh so much to say here, if you could be here to help things on the right track, and as an inspiration to some of the people here who haven't yet met you through me. And my dearest, our time together is so brief, we must seize whatever opportunity there is to be together, even if only for an hour. Please consider, and if you could come, let me know.

And remember my love (whose love?) surrounds you and draws us nearer to one another with each breath. You have the remarkable facility of becoming anyone at any time.

Love,

Carol

PS. The place where we are one is where I am with you. And here in everyday life I am with you too. There is no difference, only variations on the beauties of experience.

August 10, 1977

Dear Shamcher,

Yes, I agreed so much with the declaration - it seems overdue by many years, so to have it now may cause quite a stir. Resignation is impossible - but then how strong was the initiation tie in the first place if drugs could easily continue? And furthermore, the clarity of the body of the sufis must be

190

maintained, for otherwise it lessens in power. I see the value of opposition and how it works to strengthen the order. I want to act clearly and help further all aspects of the way, and my resistance to organization somehow works to clarify and encourage organization.

And I love you so much for all you are and all you do and all your fine work for so many years (or is it lives?)
Love forever,
Carol

August 18, 1977

Dear Carol,

Thank you for lovely letter coinciding with heavenly phone call. You are so right, so right. What more do I say? My letters seem to be so very ineffective. Words. Mean nothing/or something?
Love,
Shamcher

My dear C__,

Your letter spills over from your beautiful heart and warms and thrills me. Please do not think of your father as chronically ill. There is really no such thing. A host of busy, benevolent beings are watching, building, feeding, repairing all our organs - often hampered by limited thought patterns both from the patient himself and those around him or her. There is not a single illness or situation that hasn't been completely cured and healed by some patient - often what they call a "simple" patient, meaning that he is not always too respectful or mindful of the rules and regulations we have cluttered our minds with. People who have lost their teeth have seen new teeth grow out. Illnesses like "cancer", schizophrenia, high blood pressure, even whole limbs have been restored. And because faith is so small today, it does not happen very often. This again discourages people. Along with faith (not necessarily in some religious dogma, but faith in life and the whole universe) there are a few other things that are helpful and even necessary. Our entire civilization suffers from demanding "rights" and forgetting duties, eating hugely and eliminating insufficiently, breathing in but not wholly out, a sort of stingy feeling Gimme gimmee give me, but I won't give anything. But such simple practice as breathing all the way out until you are afraid you'll die for lack of breath gradually teaches you the balance of life. And eating good things but a bit less than you seem to "want" etc.

Love,

Shamcher

August 15, 1977

Dear Carol,

I am so completely in agreement with you, and as you say, one may look at the good intentions and respond in a polite and even loving way. Yes, I see better than ever that you are the person to continue the Message, the Order in the direction of *light* and love, unhampered by rigidity or hierarchies or titles or questionnaires or rules.

Time magazine had a weird sufi article about Hendrikus Johannes Witteveen, Managing director of the International Monetary Fund, who is a sufi. Sufis here asked me to answer or comment. First I wouldn't, knowing they wouldn't take it in. Then I reconsidered, felt it a sort of duty to try. One of the weirdest points in the *Time* article was 1923 as the date the Sufi Movement was started. Some time when we meet I may tell you of the background for this. In my reply I pretend not even to have noticed it. No time or space to go into all that.

You are the sinew and the nervous system and the sense and heart of sufism and myself, dear ever and ever Carol.

Love,

Shamcher

August 20, 1977

Dear Carol,

Your enclosed letter from our friend was very thoughtful, her trying so hard to be fair to everybody, not knowing that when Inayat Khan first met me he was delighted to have a Lao Tzu man in his message, knowing all along my endless record, knowing that I would initiate and pursue the formless, like you and so many. It is almost fate that you should be in Edmonton and so close to me and flavor the whole Canadian group as it should be flavored, for you know that with all your grace and beauty and yielding, you are still stronger, much stronger, than all of them, and in the end they will all yield.

I am very touched by your appeal to me to come there, for the time being I see no chance whatever. We are expecting the governor any day, and many others and I simply cannot leave, but whenever this situation changes I shall tell you.

If you go to the leaders camp, be honest, frank, and of course fine and diplomatic like you always are. You will suffer, but of course you will grow.

Love,

Shamcher

September 3, 1977

Dearest Shamcher,

Just received all sorts of letters from you - every time I read your letters to others, I realize that my idea of who you are is so limited, as it opens further, till I crack apart new.

Much is happening and has happened here in the past little while. Everyone is opening very very rapidly. We are coming closer and closer together - big changes for us all.

Your life is so vast and your work is so many-sided. Did you know that I was so much yearning to be with you that I almost took leave of senses entirely and came? Right to your door? But not now, how can I?

The depth of this work overwhelms and strengthens me. I know clearly that so much more is possible.

Why have I been so slow with this book? All the other books in the world will be out and gone before I manage to get things in hand and have it become a reality. What is in the way? Or is it that all things have a time?

I feel so small beside you, yet strong in your reflection. In contact with people I see that something happens and changes come - someone said I was like a midwife of the soul. I don't know what to do until I do it (or who does it?)

For years I have written to you and I have poured out all the words ever flowing. It opened a stream of prophecy so true to the heart that I still cannot but be destroyed in the process. The shining goes through all, and those who can feel it become shattered at the moment of recognition. Now I have for some time held back from writing you in the soaring way, except in matters of sufi business, which just seem to open up and express themselves in that way. But now I feel such a need to shine to you again in the true being - but words are such small versions of the great reality, which cannot be expressed except in this present life. Oh let me tell you some of the openings!

The *Koran* - I have never really read it through, but last week it opened and I read a part - where it began "We have created heaven and earth..." and I recognized the voice, the process, the truth. So much opens everywhere - but the most amazing are the people who open out! Such wonders!

People here are very close now, and we have meetings in which we do zikar (how deep it becomes) and on Thursday there are Gathas. I took Pir Vilayat's advice for a while and alternate Gathas with what he calls "Message classes" - in these I just talk and refer to Inayat Khan's presence. In all these things there is one shining star and that is the inestimable help pouring through you, and our beautiful connection. We hold Universal Worship every Sunday. We do it mostly the old way, but with a chant for each religion. What do you think? We include Native Indians as that is the original religion of this place.

You are very busy now and somehow you find the time for each individual being who comes to you. This is such beauty. How I wish I could help you, instead of being yet another, asking for help.

I am so full of such feeling that I could burst - all of it stirred by YOU. How can it be that for eternities this love flies between us as fire, smooth as water?

Love,

Carol

September 8, 1977

Dear Carol,

Thank you so much for thrilling letter crossing mine. So you were at the camp! I would have been if I hadn't had to stay at the U. but also it was as well I was not. I talked with Pir Vilayat here at Hurkalaya Sunday Sept. 4 for an hour, and you may have seen from my letters where we stood - together as usual but, there are many things I did not speak to Pir Vilayat about and you can readily guess what. Incidentally, I mentoned to him (before I even received your letter) that you had said "It is about time! May even be too late by now." To further endear you with Pir-Vilayat. Yes we spoke about the hierarchy too, in relation to the old mystic understanding and the recent physics understanding that two apparent opposites (hierarchy and no hierarchy) are really two sides of one and the same truth. Like the light photon: a wave, yes, with all the attending equations, yet, a particle, yes, with all the completely opposite attending equations. To understand this one must resort to a higher (fourth) dimension, or the quantum equations. Even very few physicists understand this yet, but the sufis should, with their term "A sufi has two points of view, his own and that of the other," (even if the other is completely opposite.)

I am not sure that Pir Vilayat was in complete agreement. He cited for me some early fight of Inayat Khan against "democratic" forces - all of which I recall very well, and it was entirely different from what I was talking about now.

But I see Pir Vilayat as one of good will who is fighting the battle with all the powers he can muster, and so I support him with all the powers I can muster.

And here is a copy of P___'s letter, to which I answered with the two letters you already received. And can you forward that letter to L__? Bless him, I think he considers starting a sufi movement-group in Calgary. And what could be better?

And since N___ seemed to want you to phone me, perhaps you might send her a letter including some of my letter copies to you, asking her please to return them to you, since you are in such good contact and since I am so lazy, or so busy, but just on your own, not ever mentioning I thought you might.

Yes, Pir Vilayat is free to say that mureeds can be removed from the order - that is his opinion. And I follow it out of compassion for Pir Vilayat. Similarly it is my understanding that no one can be removed from or retire from the order, and that this, too, is in accord with Inayat Khan, and, having once said that, I can shut my mouth and smile and say, "Of course, Pir Vilayat, you are so right." (And he is. And so am I.) And I can sign any paper Pir Vilayat puts before me, out of compassion, which is higher than "truth." For I am both Pir Vilayat and Inayat Khan and Carol. And myself? No, myself appears not to exist.
Love,
Shamcher

September 13, 1977

Dear Shamcher,

My dedication to the way of truth and whatever it can be called is so intense now, as circumstances and situations all show me so much. Because of the depth of the presence (or what can even be said?) which is so true, I know that this *inner* something must be followed, even if it should seem to contradict the rules. But whenever possible I follow the rules - many of them are the best expression.

I feel our work here to be solid, for we are based here, rooted within for guidance, rather than depending on some roving bigshot to fill us full of inspiration and then leave again. I saw the pattern of this in other cities, and it seems to weaken the individual, who feels he has little to contribute - that the main organization is something big and expensive which is an entity in itself, unreadable, instead of each one feeling responsible for the right working of the whole from his or her own heart. In the true realms this is all a child's play, but if we can reflect it a little more clearly, then part of our work will be begun.

You manage always, or almost always, to dance on the edge in that beautiful place between unformed creativity and physical manifestation.

And now someone is doing your biography! Fantastic! It will be so wonderful. I had often fantasized that I should do that some day, but realistically I can't do it now - all of life's continuous demands make it impossible. So here is one who can do it - I am very happy and look forward.

Sometimes it seems that people around me who dare to come close to me (why should I seem scary? I love them all so) seem to die or go through amazing changes. I keep them in my heart and try to help them keep open and help them "firm up" again. Is this all right?
Love,
Carol

September 12, 1977

Dear Carol,

You yourself do not actually need the papers, you know, since you are in touch with the source directly, so are continually renewed. But for proof, and for reading at Gatha classes, yes. Some in their classes read excerpts from the public message books, most of which were secret Gathas some time ago.

The "secrecy" is no longer valid and will be given up some day. Some of the "higher" Gathas though are not really needed for they talk about "difficult" mureeds and how to get rid of them - something I do not accept. The more "difficult," the more they need the message, and I have found no one yet I cannot get along with, or if I could not it would be my fault. I believe some of these "higher" Gathas were not written by Inayat Khan but by some busybody thinking he was very "high" or perhaps not thinking at all.

Carol, you will get along, with whatever papers you have or none. Of course, I should be able to create them out of space. I can do that with some important things. With "papers" I seem not able, for I cannot concentrate sharply enough on them.

Enclosed Buddha scripture was read the other day at a Universal Worship here. It is what we all need to remember. I have talked on it for a hundred years. Buddha agrees with me, I see.

Love, Carol, love,

Shamcher

September 20. 1977

Dear Carol,

You are so perfectly right in your insistence on the flow, not following more rules. Life is flow, and "being enlightened is to realize life is flow, constant change, and not to hang on to rules, fixed assets. Tradition is the opposite of enlightenment," say the sage Buddhists and sufis and yogis and ditch diggers. But you retain sufficient respect for all these to behave in patterns they can accept, so that, in time, they may listen to you and even become your mureeds, or imagine that they are your teachers.

I never follow any such thing as a topic, but talk as the moment flows or inspires me but those who like topics, let them topicer.

And what you say "rooted within" for guidance is exactly it, according to Buddha (what I sent you in last letter) and according to Inayat Khan in his latest year, and according to Lao Tzu and all the real yogis. The roving teachers are not needed or even wanted at all. None of them can reach your present pitch.

Love,

Shamcher

September 22, 1977

Dear Shamcher,

Your mention of *important* things was not overlooked.

Oh, Shamcher, I feel such a strong unrelenting aspect of my nature coming out - my personality seems to be so knowledgeable and decisive and quick and certain. I've never known this before and I hope I'm not too overbearing - in this letter and with all of my friends. It's so powerful, I feel

197

like hiding away before I tell everyone what to do and how to do it. Trying, though, to keep it in check, or should it just be? I have been this strong just today to Hidayat - I wrote I was just so moved by a feeling of him that shook and overwhelmed me.

If only I could come to see you, then this would be easy to express just by being. I was thinking that perhaps all this organization business is not for me - I should give it up because I'm at a treacherous stage. When I began it was all golden because I knew nothing. Now I see a little more in these realms, I've caught the disease of thinking that I know something. I heard myself giving a big philosophical answer to a question being so certain and sure - but was it true? Only for now, perhaps. Yet I can't quit what I am, I must refine and change and grow.

You know, I can't really conceive of your total being, so I love you in the way I can, by thinking of us as the same, of myself as you somehow. If I begin to think of the vastness of your being, I feel small and so very babylike and foolish. I could never approach you, nor expect you to even think of me, except of course from your vast incomparable kindness. But because I need so to re-establish our connection, again and again, in my heart I am you and you are me so we connect there. Then wonder of wonders, you are so vast as to be incomprehensible and you know what? So am I at the same time. But I'm still so young and barely exercised.

The only one I love is the light in us all and my whole heart, soul and being is gone to this one, whenever I see clearly that shine, that glimmer, in anyone, in anything. I can only trust where this light guides me, and in this I am totally gone. The reason why I'm writing you is to ask: why is it that when I'm not focused here doing something or being with someone, then I feel like I stretch across North America. I literally feel that I am a blanket lying over the continent. Or else my exploration is inner, and what worlds there are! What is this? And the loves I feel break and elate my heart.

Rosie will be one year old tomorrow. How I love her! I can't begin to tell you. Oh dearest friend and self, thank you so much for everything.
Love,
Carol

September 27, 1977

Yes, dear, dear Carol, it must be you. You who starts this new group accepting all, as I explain in enclosed letter to G__. You do it as the "flow" tells you, when it tells you. You know, don't you? This is why you had such urge to have all Gathas and Githas and Sangathas and Sangithas. So many of originally secret Gathas have come into the books. And your books, and my books. And our minds and hearts.

Oh, Carol, you blessed one, what an enormous task is yours! and yet so easy.

Love,

Shamcher

September 27, 1977

Dear G___,

Thank you for inspiring letter. Since you want to see my folly with the fortune teller (and hers) though it may be a little unfair to call her a fortune teller, I submit it with my apologies. A lot of sufis go to her to weaken their intuition and ability to think and act.

Also I enclose two recent letters to Pir Vilayat. The first has had wide publicity and you may show it to anyone you want. The second is so far restricted to a few close friends. For one thing, I don't want to hurt or upset the fine Sam Lewis disciples, who already complain that I should restrict my words, and I reply, "Yes, you are so right. Maybe I should not come to your meetings at all." "Oh yes, Shamcher, you must come, and speak as you want of course, we just want you to be a bit careful." "Yes, Sir, I will try, however maybe what I feel must be said is exactly what you consider careless, so what do we do???"

But actually G___, new organizations, less "organized", will spring up now, for neither Pir Vilayat's "Sufi Order" nor SIRS (Sam's) are fulfilling their purpose, not sufficiently. So a loosely knit group will form that recognizes all but are not committed to either or any or their rules and declarations and words. With supreme bliss and love they attend to *all* of any or no-organization, and express respect but not obedience to teachers and non-teachers, and I believe this will come from Canada, for it is time Canada took the initiative after all the follies we in the states have perpetrated.

Love,

Shamcher

September 28, 1977

Dearest Carol,

Thank you for great letter. No, I was not exaggerating. Your enclosed letter - the part about stretching across the whole North American continent should be in your book. So neatly fit into your role outlined in yesterday's letter. With your new role, with your organization, only your rules (if any) matter, except that, of course, you'll try to be polite or rather considerate. Even when others may not be. Oh, your feeling of being so wide and strong - just received the same day I had written you about your new role. Phenomenal.

I don't think you should yet talk to anyone about it, only those you are sure would understand, perhaps nobody, perhaps two or three. As you feel. And what am I doing? Daring to advise? Silly of me. Forgive.

Love and admiration,

Shamcher

September 27, 1977

Dear Shamcher,

Thank you for all the fine letters I have been receiving from you lately - I hope you know how good for me (and all) they are - and all your guiding thoughts. I can see that I must keep a part of myself always a little apart from those who come to me, not that I don't give all, and entirely, but to keep a bit apart to keep my own rhythm, to ensure that they learn a higher form, to bring it higher rather than to burn up in the first flare - this thought is not easily expressed.

I haven't much time to write just now. Forgive me please for all the pain I have caused you by my foolish actions as I learn my way here. And thank you for all your support and help and sustenance.

Love,

Carol

September 30, 1977

Dear Shamcher,

Your letter with the other letters came just now and I am quite overcome by the message contained there. But you know me well enough to know that all you say is already in my heart. It seems inevitable that as I further dedicate myself to this way that the responsibilities will increase, and with that the wonders! I have no words at all for the moving feelings within me and so I can simply send all these feelings to you and to all in gratitude and wonder at all that has come and the joy of being able to do this.

It seems best that I can only see the next step ahead rather than the total view (or do I have that too?) If I were to have the total picture there wouldn't be the fun of discovering it all over again and again. There is more to say than words, and you know all I mean to say in your dear deep heart.
Love,
Carol

October 6, 1977

Dearest Carol,

Oh, Carol, I am so deeply grateful that you realize the need for this new body (or may we call it "organization"?) to form itself quietly, without any pushing - to accept all, to never talk about "how difficult some mureeds are." No, only one in our lives can be difficult: ourselves. This new organization will be open arms, accepting all, criminals, smokers, drinkers, - the worse, the more they need us. There has, in the ancient sufi organizations, been all kinds of tendencies, fine and not so fine. Now, at this time, we need to purify the trend - not by excluding whom we haughtily consider impure, by accepting and purifying all. You have proven able to personify this.

No use being an "organizer", that's not what we need. We need a heart. That's you.

Your beautiful letter, and the letter to you - all show that you are the person.
Love
Shamcher

October 13, 1977

Dear Carol,

Here are your precious letters and my towering love and intolerable watching over and under you all day and night, seeing all you do and think, learning from it, mounting mountains in ecstacy, writhing in pain sometimes, and learning even more from that. Oh how you drag me and ease me and comfort me through life's boulevards and avenues and alleys and tunnels and the narrowest channels and make me feel and think and know and not know.
Love, Carol, yes, during the entire eternal NOW.
Shamcher

November 10, 1977

My dear eternal Carol,

Really, Carol, no person can "represent" me to you. We are closer than my own mind is to my body or soul. And for your beautiful and exquisite letter to Hidayat and to me my eternal thanks. We had a meeting after two days of seminar here with Pir Vilayat, when I was asked to wind up the meeting. I first stressed the present world movement about drugs, their danger to Pir's residence both in France and here, then asked Pir if, not merely old Shamcher but any one could not, if they wished, be a member of both the Sufi Order and SIRS. Yes yes said Pir, conditioned on that they give up drugs. So now you know.

Carol I think the time has come for you to sign and send out a declaration: I give my idea, and you correct it and, if you are very kind, you send it back to me so I can see it before you publish it. Here is my vague idea:

"We the undersigned sufis of Edmonton, in the province of Alberta in Canada reached the sufi world through the message of Inayat Khan. So we are a nucleus of the Brotherhood of all beings united in THE ONLY BEING, humans, animals, plants, bacterias, all other beings including the events appearing as bodies or objects, on earth, in the solar system, the galaxies, the entire universe.

We are members of the Sufi Order headed by Pir-Vilayat and accept as equal members all of this order and respect the tenets of that order at all times. Pir Vilayat was the initiator of some of us. We equally are members of the Federation of Sufi Groups formed under the friendship-guidance of Hidayat Khan and all members of these groups are members with equal right accepted by us. We honor and accept as teachers Neeatma Paloheimo and all other beloved teachers and /or sufis. We equally are members of SIRS based in San Francisco and established by Samuel Lewis and now headed by Moineddin Jablonski and all members of this organization are accepted equally with us.

We are members of and accept the members of each and every sufi group in the world, every religious group, every group of any other character, every individual of any type, human, animal, plant, mineral, or in terms of modern physics: event. All these form the brotherhood in the fatherhood of God.

All titles, all ideas, all structures of any mind are respected and

honored by us, though not held sacred. Only ONE is sacred: THE ONLY BEING."
Love,
Shamcher

Undated

(Sabira will read this at a Mureed meeting which I shall not attend..)

Shamcher wants to thank you-all for your invitation to him to join in this meeting, and he much regrets that he couldn't come. He has nothing to say that you do not all know already, so here it is:

What we call the Sufi Message has been known by a few sufis and others throughout the entire history of sufism and the world. and is constantly beamed from the joyful void or womb of Space to any attentive listener, whatever happens to the organizations we form or sometimes deform to the best or next-best of our abilities.

We-all know that, helped by beloved teachers, or just on our own, we may tune in to this stream of inspiration, of love, harmony and beauty, of knowledge and insight, which we call the message. Some like to identify it with Inayat Khan, or with other persons, or with no person. Some think it all started with one specific person or messenger, and their belief should be respected if not necessarily followed. Others see it as a lovely aspect of the space-continuum itself, ever present, from eternity to eternity, nobody's specific possession. If some want to fight for one or the other concept, we hope not too many will be too badly hurt, or if hurt they be, that they may be healed again.

Allah Ho Akbar, Halleluya, Kyrie Eleison, Patanjali's Yoga Sutras, the Tao of Physics. And now, for Buddha's farewell address:

THE GOSPEL OF BUDDHA - Buddha's Farewell Address
"....It is only, Ananda, when the Tathagata, ceasing to attend to any outward thing, becomes plunged in that devout meditation of heart which is concerned with no bodily object, it is only then that the body of the Tathagata is at ease.
Therefore, O Ananda, be ye lamps unto yourselves and do not rely on external help.
Rely on yourselves,

Hold fast to the truth as a lamp. Seek salvation alone in the truth. Look not for assistance to anyone beside yourselves.

And how, Ananda, can a brother be a lamp unto himself, rely on himself only and not on any external help, holding fast to the truth as his lamp and seeking salvation in the truth alone, looking not for assistance to anyone beside himself?

Those who, either now or after I am dead, shall be a lamp unto themselves, relying upon themselves only and not relying upon any external help, but holding fast to the truth as their lamp, and seeking their salvation in the truth alone, shall not look for assistance to anyone beside themselves, it is they, Ananda, among my bhikshus, who shall reach the very topmost height ! But they must be anxious to learn."

EPILOGUE

Shamcher spent the remainder of his years working non-stop to promote Ocean Thermal Energy Conversion (OTEC). The letters he and I frequently exchanged continued until January, 1980, when I found I could no longer write to him. We phoned from time to time, but written contact was over. I believe it was a preparation. Shamcher passed away on April 29, 1980 in Berkeley, California.

From then on we met only in intuition. For some time I thought it would be possible to have a similar experience with others, but over the years I have discovered that this relationship was truly unique. Completing these letters to be shared once again has revealed a new facet of Shamcher's gift to me. Not only have I been in touch again with the remarkable promise that our communications fostered, I also see that he took me through the darkest portals into a life of light and hope. Relying on Shamcher, I was able to heal my heart at the highest level after the death of my son, by exploring the journey of mystical awareness and purpose that Shamcher's loving being brought to me.

The letters in this book cover that time until the granting of my heart's desire: to have another child. I am so grateful that Rosie came into my life. Simply by her presence she taught me to live again. She arrived as a truly divine gift and the joy I now have as a grandmother with her children is pure and sweet.

By being involved in the sustaining current of the Sufi Message I was able to live a new life, and in gratitude for that gift I worked joyfully in sufi organization and creating community for many years.

Life holds many surprises as the soul finds its fulfillment on earth. For me, finding the intuitive current of contact with Shamcher eventually led me to discover talents and interests I could use to help humanity, not only in the inner world of sufi orders, but in the day to day world of life on earth.

Many of my dear sufi friends now form the foundation of the Sufi Movement in Canada, while others find their spiritual home in the Sufi Order International or the Ruhaniat. Still others have been guided to work in the world, while retaining the protection of God in their hearts.

ACKNOWLEDGEMENTS

I am very grateful for the support and encouragement I've received in the publication of these letters. Many thanks to divine Diane Feught for her beautiful cover design; to generous Joe Clare for his inspiration, encouragement and moral support; and to graceful Nancy Mortifee for helping me stay on track. For helping me approach this material with a new perspective, warm thanks to Ann Mortifee, Tanis Helliwell, Jim Van Wyck, Bill Annett, Amidha Porter, Carol Sokoloff and Forest Shomer.

Particularly special thanks to my intuitive, creative, God-given husband, James K-M, in whose presence I found the energy and clarity to complete this work.

To all the dear friends who helped and encouraged the first photocopied version of this book of letters, back in 1980, thank you so very much. I can't name you all here for the list would be too long, but you know who you are. Thank you for living this process with me at that time. I'm honoured and humbled. Special thanks beyond words to Gary and Rosie Sill.

Editorial Note: Most of the letters are presented here as they were written, with few omissions. I trust privacy has been protected, and many names have been removed, except with public figures like Pir Vilayat or Hidayat. Gaps in the correspondence are due to letters not found or phone calls that weren't documented. Shamcher's originals were typed and have been edited for spelling and typos, and my hand-written originals were lightly edited for clarity.

Now, so many years later, I let all the letters pass from my hands, watching the pages float away on the surface of the river, carried by the current to dissolve in the sea.

Carol Sill, Vancouver BC, 2011

For background to the book, photos, comments, links, and contact info,
see the website at http://www.letters.shamcher.com

11108916R00135